THE ULTIMATE
GEOGRAPHY
— QUIZ BOOK —

TEST YOUR KNOWLEDGE OF THE WORLD WITH 720 CHALLENGING MULTIPLE CHOICE QUESTIONS!

B.C. LESTER B

D0291222

While every precaution has been taken in the making ⌐⌐⌐⌐⌐ ⌐⌐⌐ ⌐ssumes no
responsibility for errors, or for damages resulting from ⌐⌐⌐⌐⌐ ⌐⌐⌐ormation contained
herein. No part of this book may be copied, reproduced or sold without the express permission
from the copyright owner.
Copyright B.C. Lester Books 2020. All rightes reserved.

A QUICK MESSAGE FROM THE PUBLISHER...

THANKS FOR PURCHASING THIS BOOK...

...we really hope you enjoy it. If you have the chance, then all feedback on Amazon is greatly appreciated. We have put a lot of effort into making this book, so if you are not completely satisfied, please email us at ben@bclesterbooks.com and we will do our best to address any issues. If you have any suggestions, want to get in touch or want to send us your score, then email at the same address - ben@bclesterbooks.com

IS THIS BOOK MISPRINTED?

Printing presses, like humans, aren't quite perfect. Send us an email at ben@bclesterbooks.com with a photo of the misprint, and we will get another copy sent out to you!

WHO ARE WE AT B.C. LESTER BOOKS?

B.C. Lester Books is a small publishing firm of three people based in Buckinghamshire, UK. We aim to provide quality works in all things geography, for kids and adults, with varying interests. We have already released a selection of activity, trivia and fact books and are working hard to bring you wider selection. Have a suggestion for us? Then email ben@bclesterbooks.com. We are all ears!

IF YOU LIKED THIS TITLE, YOU MAY LIKE THESE!

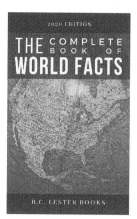

Detailed facts of the world, it's countries and geography.

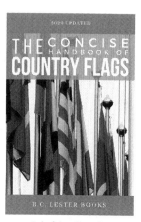

Colorful and concise guide to country flags and facts.

THE GEOGRAPHY QUIZ

Tackle the challenge solo or with friends and family! Good Luck!

Answers start at Page 78

Note: *There are 40 answers per page at the rear of this book. We therefore recommend you check your answers after every 40 questions if you are quizzing alone; so as to not spoil other questions!*

TOTAL SCORE

/720

1 **In which country is the Sinai peninsula located?**
   A Israel   C Turkey
   B Egypt   D Saudi Arabia

2 **In which continent can you find the country of Palau?**
   A Asia   C Australia & Oceania
   B Africa   D Antarctica

3 **If one were to sail from Sapporo to Vladivostok, what sea would they cross to make this journey?**
   A Yellow Sea   C Sea of Korea
   B Sea of Okhotsk   D Sea of Japan

4 **To the nearest 1000 miles, what is the distance from London to New York?**
   A 3000 miles   C 5000 miles
   B 4000 miles   D 6000 miles

5 **What is the deepest part of the Mediterranean sea?**
   A Wellington Trench   C Calypso Deep
   B Athenas Deep   D Adriana Deep

6 **In which country is Mount Athos located in?**
   A Albania   C Italy
   B Greece   D Turkey

7 **Which U.S. state is located directly north of Maryland?**
   A New York   C Delaware
   B Virginia   D Pennsylvania

8 **Which ocean has the longest border with the USA?**
   A Pacific Ocean   C Atlantic Ocean
   B Arctic Ocean   D Indian Ocean

9 **What was the largest empire in history?**
   A British Empire   C Russian Empire
   B Mongol Empire   D Roman Empire

10 **Brooklyn, a district of New York, is named after the village of Breukelen, located in which country?**
   A Netherlands   C Germany
   B Sweden   D Denmark

11 **The Faroe Islands is governed by which sovereign nation?**
A United Kingdom   **C** Denmark
B Iceland   **D** Norway

12 **The River Danube crosses how many countries?** *The most in the world*
A 4 *Germany Austria*   **C** 8 *Romania Bulgaria*
B 6 *slovakia Hungary*   **D** 10 *Moldova Ukraine*
Croatia Serbia

13 **What is the second largest island in the world?**
A Honshu   **C** Borneo
B New Guinea   **D** Madagascar

14 **Moscow sits on which river?**
A Ural River   **C** Moskva River
B Volga   **D** Don

15 **What country beginning with B has the longest border with France?**
A Belgium   **C** Britain
B Belarus   **D** Brazil *(via French Guiana)*

16 **What R is the official currency on Saudi Arabia?**
A Riyal   **C** Rupee
B Real   **D** Riyadh

17 **Which 3 countries have a Hindu majority population?**
A India, Nepal, Mauritius   **C** India, Sri Lanka, Maldives
B India, Nepal, Sri Lanka   **D** India, Nepal, Bangladesh

18 **How many countries does Indonesia share a land border with?** *East Timor, Papua New Guinea*
A 1   **C** 3
B 2 *Malasia*   **D** 4

19 **After Brazil, what is the second largest country in South America?**
A Colombia   **C** Peru
B Argentina   **D** Venezuela

20 **Which English city has more miles of canals than Venice?**
A Birmingham   **C** Milton Keynes
B Manchester   **D** Liverpool

10 /20

21 Mount Vesuvius overlooks which modern Italian city?

A Catania
B Palermo
C Rome
D Naples

22 The Seychelles are located in which ocean?

A Pacific Ocean
B Indian Ocean
C Atlantic Ocean
D Arctic Ocean

23 The only U.S. state to have one syllable in it's name begins with which letter?

A A
B C
C M   *MAINE*
D N

24 Before the Euro, what was the currency of Greece?

A Drachma
B Lira
C Mark
D Shekel

25 What are Japanese Shinkansen better known as?

A Sushi
B Bullet Trains
C Zen Temples
D Type of Rice

26 What is the most southerly capital city in South America?

A Buenos Aires
B Brasilia
C Montevideo   *URUGUAY*
D Santiago

27 Which country has the longest coastline in the world?

A Canada
B Russia
C Indonesia
D Norway

28 Which river flows through Paris?

A Rhone
B Rhine
C Loire
D Seine

29 Alnwick Castle in England is used for the exterior shots in which film series?

A Lord Of The Rings
B Harry Potter
C Jack And The Beanstalk
D The Castle

30 Which country has the capital, Sofia?

A Kosovo
B North Macedonia
C Romania
D Bulgaria

31 Which European capital was built across 14 islands?

A Amsterdam
B Stockholm
C Copenhagen
D Helsinki

32 What does the 'DC' stand for in Washington DC?

A District Capitol
B District of Columbia
C District Captial
D District of the Commonwealth

33 Petra, an acient city is located in which modern country?

A Saudi Arabia
B Iraq
C Jordan
D Israel

34 By what name is the parallel of latitude 23.5 degrees North of the equator commonly known?

A Tropic of Cancer
B Tropic of Capricorn
C Tropic of Aries
D Tropic of Virgo

35 Pho and banh mi are dishes from which country?

A Thailand
B Cambodia
C Vietnam
D China

36 Which U.S. state shares the name of the North American territory held by France until 1803?

A Iowa
B Michigan
C Arkansas
D Louisiana

37 The Great Barrier Reef is off the coast of which Australian state?

A New South Wales
B Queensland
C Victoria
D Western Australia

38 Victoria Falls is located on the border of Zambia and which other African country?

A South Africa
B Mozambique
C Zimbabwe
D Malawi

355 feet

39 What is the world's largest island?

A Greenland
B Australia
C New Guinea
D Borneo

40 Bermuda is an overseas dependency of which country?

A United States
B Portugal
C Spain
D United Kingdom

41 To the nearest 1000 miles, what is the distance from Los Angeles to Tokyo?

A 3000 miles
B 4000 miles
C 5000 miles
D 6000 miles

42 After the Nile and Amazon, what is the third longest river in the world?

A Congo River
B Yellow River
C Yangtze
D Mississippi River

43 Mount Rushmore is located in which U.S. state?

A South Dakota
B North Dakota
C Wyoming
D Montana

44 The AT&T football stadium is located is which U.S. city?

A Phoenix
B Dallas
C Denver
D Los Angeles

45 Tropical grassland is another name for which biome?

A Serengeti
B Shrubland
C Savanna
D Steppe

46 The extinct Dodo was once only found on which island country beginning with M?

A Mauritius
B Madagascar
C Maldives
D Marshall Islands

47 On a list of U.S. states from largest to smallest in size, with 1st being largest, California is where?

A 2nd
B 3rd
C 4th
D 5th

Alaska Texas

48 The construction of the Eiffel Tower was completed in which decade?

A 1860s
B 1870s
C 1880s
D 1890s

49 How many countries have Arabic as their official language?

A 6 countries
B 16 countries
C 26 countries
D 36 countries

50 What is the largest desert in the world?

A Sahara Desert
B The Arctic Desert
C Gobi Desert
D Antarctica

51 How many capital cities does South Africa have?
A 1   *Capetown*   C 3   *Pretoria*
B 2   D 4
Bloemfontein

52 Which Scottish Loch is the largest, and home to
Scottish folklore of a monster?
A Loch Ness   C Loch Lochy
B Loch Aviemore   D Loch Leven

53 The Eurostar connects which London train station to
mainland Europe?
A Paddington Station   C London Waterloo
B King's Cross Station   D London St. Pancras

54 How many provinces does Canada have? *British Columbia*
A 7 *Alberta   Manitoba*   C 13 *Quebec   New Brunswick*
B 10 *Saskatchewan   Ontario*   D 16 *Nova Scotia PEI Newfundland*

55 Guinea is present in how many country names?
A 1 *Equatorial New G*   C 3 *G*
B 2   D 4
G - Bissau   *Papau New G*

56 How many time zones does Russia span?
A 1   C 11
B 6   D 16

57 What dialect of Chinese is spoken in Hong Kong?
A Cantonese   C Taiwanese
B Mandarin   D Taishanese

58 The Russian language uses which alphabet?
A Russian   C Latin
B Cyrillic   D Orthodox

59 What is the denonym of people from Cyprus (what do
you call someone from Cyprus)?
A Cyprite   C Cyprish
B Cyprusian   D Cypriot

60 Along with Spanish, what other language is the official
language of Ibiza (and the Balearic Islands)?
A Occitan   C Catalan
B Greek   D Basque

61 **Bahrain and Qatar are countries bordering which body of water?**

A Arabian Sea
B Persian Gulf / Arabian Gulf
C Red Sea
D Gulf Of Oman

62 **Upper Volta was the name of which modern country?**

A Mali
B Niger
C Burkina Faso
D Sierra Leone

63 **Lake Victoria in Africa spans which countries?**

A Tanzania, Uganda, Kenya
B Tanzania, Kenya, Rwanda
C Kenya, Uganda, Rwanda
D Kenya, Uganda, Burundi

64 **How many time zones does China span?**

A 1
B 4
C 7
D 10

65 **Angel Falls, the tallest waterfall in the world is located in which country?**

A Zimbabwe
B Canada
C Venezuela
D Brazil

3,212 ft

66 **Which of the Great Lakes is the only one that is completely in the USA?**

A Lake Huron
B Lake Superior
C Lake Erie
D Lake Michigan

67 **What is the capital of the U.S. state of Kentucky?**

A Louisville
B Frankfort
C Charleston
D Lexington

68 **What is the only U.S. state that borders the Great Lakes and Atlantic Ocean?**

A New Hampshire
B Pennsylvania
C New York State
D Massachusetts

69 **What is the largest city in the Canadian territory of Nanuvut?**

A Igloolik
B Ivujivik
C Iqaluit
D Churchill

70 **The Great Pyramids of Giza are nearest to which Egyptian city?**

A Giza
B 6th of October City
C Gaza
D Cairo

71 Ceuta and Mellila are African cities belonging to which European country?
A Portugal   C Greece
B Spain   D Cyprus

72 Osaka in Japan is located on which Japanese island?
A Honshu   C Shikoku
B Kyushu   D Okinawa

73 How many islands does Indonesia have, to the nearest 1000?
A 1,800   C 18,000
B 6,000   D 60,000

74 What is the most spoken language in India?
A Gujarat   C Sanskrit
B English   D Hindi

75 What country was formerly known as 'East Pakistan'?
A Pakistan   C Myanmar (Burma)
B Bangladesh   D Afghanistan

76 In which year was the Soviet Union formed?
A 1915   C 1919
B 1917   D 1939

77 What is the official demonym for someone who lives in Massachusetts?
A Bay Stater   C New Englander
B Massachusettian   D Massachusite

78 The region of Transylvania belongs to which country?
A Hungary   C Ukraine
B Serbia   D Romania

79 Yellowstone National Park may be found mainly in which U.S. state?
A Utah   C Wyoming
B Idaho   D Montana

80 What is the height of the highest point of the Maldives?
A 3m (10ft)   C 10m (32ft)
B 5m (16ft)   D 18m (60ft)

81 The San Andreas Fault in the United States is an example of what type of plate boundary?

A Convergent Plate Boundary   C Transform Plate Boundary
B Alternating Plate Boundary   D Diverging Plate Boundary

82 The Appalachian Mountains has it's highest point in which U.S. state?

A North Carolina   C Virginia
B South Carolina   D Maine

83 What town is the highest permanently settled place in the world?

A Lhasa   C La Paz
B La Rinconada   D Thimphu

84 Which country dedicated their name to an Italian explorer?

A Peru   C St. Lucia
B Marshall Islands   D Colombia

85 The Juventus football team is found in which Italian city?

A Venice   C Genoa
B Turin   D Florence

86 Alpacas are native to which continent?

A South America   C Africa
B North America   D Australia & Oceania

87 Which New York Boroughs are situated on Long Island?

A Brooklyn & Staten Island   C Brooklyn & Queens
B Queens & Staten Island   D The Bronx & Queens

88 How many countries border the Red Sea?

A 3 Saudi Arabia   Yemen   C 9 Eritrea
B 6 Egypt Sudan   D 12 Djibouti

89 Zaire is the former name for which country?

A Democratic Republic Of Congo   C Republic of The Congo
B Central African Republic   D Cameroon

90 Which city is the highest capital city in terms of altitude?

A Bogota, Colombia   C Thimphu, Bhutan
B Quito, Ecuador   D La Paz, Bolivia

91 **The Pyrennes are a mountain range that separates which 2 countries?**
A Greece & Albania
B France & Spain
C Russia & Georgia
D Turkey & Armenia

92 **Mecca and Medina are situated in which country?**
A Jordan
B Palestine
C Iraq
D Saudi Arabia

93 **How many countries begin with the letter N?**
A 5
B 10
C 15
D 20

94 **What D is the capital of East Timor (Timor-Leste)?**
A Dilbutan
B Dili
C Dharma
D Dhaka

95 **What is the largest Australian state?**
A Northern Territories
B Western Australia
C Queensland
D Victoria

96 **A is a record-breaking village with the shortest name in the world. Which country is it located in?**
A Norway
B Iceland
C Russia
D Switzerland

97 **Mount Chimborazo is the closest mountain to space. Which country is it in?**
A Kenya
B Indonesia
C Ecuador
D Tanzania

98 **What is the longest river in the UK?**
A River Severn
B River Thames
C River Trent
D River Tyne

99 **What is the deepest freshwater lake in the world?**
A Lake Lagoda
B Great Bear lake
C Lake Superior
D Lake Baikal

100 **What is the longest river in North America?**
A Missouri River
B St. Lawrence River
C Mississippi River
D Rio Grande

/20

101 The Gobi Desert is situated in which countries?
A South Africa, Botswana, Namibia   C China & Mongolia
B Iran, Turkmenistan, Afghanistan   D Syria, Turkey, Iraq

102 The second highest mountain is the world is the highest point of which country?
A China   C India
B Bhutan   D Pakistan

103 If you were to travel from Mexico to Colombia by land, whats the minimum amount of countries you would need to pass? *El Salvador,*
A 4   C 6
B 5   D 7

104 The State of Amazonas is the largest state of which country?
A Peru   C Guyana
B Colombia   D Brazil

105 The southernmost tip of South America belongs to which country?
A United Kingdom   C Chile
B Argentina   D Norway

106 To get from Malaysia to Russia by land, whats the minimum number of countries you would need to pass?
A 2   C 4
B 3   D 5

107 The Kuril Islands are an archipelago that belong to which country?
A Japan   C Russia
B United States   D Finland

108 What is the name of France's largest island?
A Corsica   C Guadeloupe
B Sardinia   D New Caledonia

109 Tristan De Cunha is a remote island that is closest to which mainland country?
A South Africa   C Argentina
B Namibia   D Brazil

110 The Tanjung Puting is a national park in which country?
A Thailand   C Philippines
B Indonesia   D Malaysia

111 **Australia became nominally independent from the UK in which year?**
A 1897
B 1901
C 1907
D 1921

112 **Greenland, an autonomous region of Denmark, is how many times bigger than Denmark proper (excluding Greenland)?**
A 5 times
B 10 times
C 20 times
D 50 times

113 **What is the name of Indonesia's most populous island?**
A Sumatra
B Java
C Sulawesi
D Bali

114 **What is the capital of Mongolia?**
A Almaty
B Ulaan Ude
C Ulaan Baatar
D Erdenet

115 **The Taj Mahal may be found in which Indian state?**
A Maharashtra
B Rajasthan
C Gujarat
D Uttar Pradesh

116 **How many Nordic countries are there?**
A 4
B 5
C 6
D 7

117 **The exclave Russian oblast, Kaliningrad, borders which two countries?**
A Lithuania & Poland
B Lithuania & Belarus
C Poland & Belarus
D Lithuania & Latvia

118 **The Antilles are a group of islands in which region of the world?**
A Caribbean
B Mediterranean
C Southeast Asia
D Pacific

119 **The islands of the Caribbean are also known by which name?**
A Lucayan Islands
B Central American Islands
C West Indies
D Antilles

120 **In 1804, which Caribbean nation was established after a successful slave revolt?**
A Dominica
B Haiti
C Grenada
D Cuba

/20

121 **The city of Paris is in which of the 13 French regions?**
A Ile De France   C Centre Val De Loire
B Hauts De France   D Grand Est

122 **Which city has a water feature called the Jet d'eau, jetting lake water vertically over 50 metres?**
A Montreal   C Geneva
B Lausanne   D Annecy

123 **What is the name of the highest mountain in Switzerland?**
A Mont Blanc   C Matterhorn
B Grossglockner   D Dufourspitze

124 **What is the name of the valley of Northern Italy, where the city of Milan is situated?**
A Bologna Valley   C Brescia Valley
B Po Valley   D Parma Valley

125 **What is the capital of Benin?**
A Porto-Novo   C Tamale
B Lome   D Ouagadougou

126 **How many countries does the continent of Africa contain?**
A 34   C 54
B 44   D 64

127 **The Mediterranean Sea borders which continents?**
A Africa, Europe   C Africa, Middle East, Europe
B Africa, Asia, Europe   D Europe

128 **What strait in Turkey separates Asia from Europe?**
A Aegean Strait   C Constantinople
B Marmara Strait   D The Bosphorus

129 **What is Taiwan's official name?**
A Republic of Taiwan   C Republic of China
B Formosa   D South Japan

130 **The Ottoman Empire existed until 1922, preluding which country's war of independence?**
A Armenia   C Turkey
B Saudi Arabia   D Greece

131 The Statue of Liberty was built in what decade?
A 1860s   C 1880s
B 1870s   D 1890s

132 The Burj Al Arab is a 5 star hotel in what city?
A Doha   C Abu Dhabi
B Dubai   D Riyadh

133 Babylon is an ancient city that is located in which modern day country?
A Iran   C Greece
B Turkey   D Iraq

134 Which is the only Ancient 7 wonders of the world to largely still exist today?
A Machu Picchu   C Angkor Wat
B Great Pyramids of Giza   D Petra

135 Which from the flags of Poland, Indonesia and Monaco has the white stripe displayed on the top half?
A Poland   C Indonesia
B Monaco   D None of them

136 The flag of Romania is almost identical to the flag of which other country?
A Colombia   C Chad
B Senegal   D Ecuador

137 The flag of Ireland is almost identical to the horizontally flipped flag of which country?
A Cote D'Ivoire   C Laos
B Sierra Leone   D Vanuatu

138 Which flag color appears most often of the 196 sovereign nation flags?
A Black   C Blue
B White   D Red

139 What is the only country flag in the world that has more than 4 sides?
A Micronesia   C Kyrgyzstan
B Sao Tome and Principe   D Nepal

140 What is the smallest U.S. state?
A Connecticut   C Vermont
B Rhode Island   D Delaware

/20

141 What flag color typically symbolises Islam?

A Black   C White
B Green   D Red

142 What are the Pan-African flag colors?

A Blue, White   C Green, Yellow, Red
B Green, Red   D Black, White, Green, Red

143 Silesia is a region in which country?

A Czech Republic   C Germany
B Poland   D Austria

144 What is the largest island that belongs to Scotland, excluding Great Britain itself?

A Isle of Lewis   C Isle of Harris
B Isle of Mull   D Isle of Skye

145 What is the capital of the Faroe Islands?

A Beerensburg   C Lerwick
B Klaksvik   D Torshavn

146 The Isle of Wight in the UK belongs in which county?

A Isle of Wight   C Dorset
B Hampshire   D Sussex

147 What is the shortest distance in the English Channel between Great Britain and France?

A 6 miles   C 46 miles
B 26 miles   D 66 miles

148 Bodensee is a lake that borders what 3 countries?

A Poland, Czech Republic, Slovakia   C Germany, Switzerland, Austria
B Austria, Hungary, Slovenia   D Germany, Belgium, Netherlands

149 German is an official language in how many countries?

A 3   C 9
B 6   D 12

150 What is the largest sized disputed sovereign nation?

A Antarctica   C Russia
B China   D Cyprus

151 Madeira is an island in the Atlantic Ocean, belonging to which country?
A Portugal   C Greece
B Italy   D Spain

152 What is the major export commodity for Iran, Saudi Arabia and the United Arab Emirates?
A Sand   C Pharmaceuticals
B Oil   D Electronics

153 The Oriental Pearl TV tower is located in which city?
A Hong Kong   C Shanghai
B Guangzhou   D Beijing

154 Hawaii is home to the tallest mountain in the world when measured from the ocean floor. How tall is it?
A 9200m   C 11200m
B 10200m   D 12200m

155 What is the name of the highest mountain in the Balkans?
A Musala   C Mt. Korab
B Mt. Olympus   D Mt. Elbrus

156 The Marina Bay Sands Hotel is located in which city?
A Jakarta   C Singapore
B Kuala Lumpur   D Hong Kong

157 Which country has the shortest coastline in the world?
A Bosnia & Herzegovina   C Jordan
B Democratic Republic of Congo   D Monaco

158 The town of Neum is the largest settlement along the short coastline of which country?
A Bosnia & Herzegovina   C Jordan
B Democratic Republic of Congo   D Monaco

159 What is the highest mountain of the Iberian peninsula called?
A Teide   C Mulhacen
B Aneto   D Moncayo

160 Before the Euro, what currency was used by Spain?
A Franc   C Real
B Peso   D Peseta

/20

161 Dakar is located on the most westerly point of mainland Africa, in which country?

A Senegal   C The Gambia
B Guinea   D Sierra Leone

162 Haile Selassie was emperor of which African country?

A Kenya   C Ethiopia
B Tanzania   D Zaire

163 The Anatolia peninsula is located in which country?

A Greece   C Russia
B Turkey   D Iran

164 The ancient city of Carthage is located in which modern day country?

A Libya   C Egypt
B Italy   D Tunisia

165 In 1867, the U.S. purchased Alaska from who?

A Native Inuits   C Russia
B United Kingdom   D Canada

166 Tahiti is an island in which overseas territory?

A American Samoa   C Pitcairn Islands
B Cook Islands   D French Polynesia

167 New Britain and New Ireland are islands of which country?

A Tanzania   C Papua New Guinea
B New Zealand   D Solomon Islands

168 The Levant is a region of which geographical region?

A Central Asia   C North Africa
B Middle East   D East Africa

169 What is the most northernly city in China?

A Mohe City   C Urumqi
B Harbin   D Jiagedaqi

170 Which country has the shortest land border with Russia?

A Lithuania   C North Korea
B Norway   D United States

171 How many mountains are above 8000m?
    A 4   **C** 24
    B 14   **D** 34

172 What is the largest active volcano in Europe?
    A Mt. Elbrus   **C** Mt. Vesuvius
    B Eyjafjallajökull   **D** Mt. Etna

173 What is the most northerly settlement in the U.S.?
    A Utqiagvik   **C** Prudhoe Bay
    B Alert   **D** Resolute

174 The Sherpa people are indigenous to which mountain range?
    A Tian Shan   **C** Hindu Kush
    B Himalayas   **D** Tibetian

175 Known for it's tea and silk, Assam is a province in which country?
    A Bangladesh   **C** India
    B China   **D** Myanmar

176 Judaism is the majority religious affiliation of how many countries?
    A 0   **C** 2
    B 1   **D** 3

177 What is the official currency in the Maldives?
    A Riyal   **C** Rufiyaa
    B Rupee   **D** Rupiah

178 What is the official language in Malta?
    A Maltese   **C** English
    B Italian   **D** Sicilian

179 The Sahara desert may be found in how many countries?
    A 5   **C** 15
    B 10   **D** 20

180 What is the capital of Oman?
    A Aden   **C** Muscat
    B Salalah   **D** Sana'a

/20

181 What is the most southerly city in Africa?

A Port Elizabeth   C Johannesburg
B Cape Town   D George

182 What city of India used to be called Madras?

A Madurai   C Chennai
B Kolkata   D Ahmedabad

183 The Titanic sailed form which city?

A Liverpool   C Bristol
B London   D Southampton

184 Japan attached Pearl Harbor in 1941 on which American island?

A Midway Atoll   C Oahu
B Hawaii   D Guam

185 The assassination of Archduke Franz Ferdinand in 1914 created tension between Austria-Hungary and which other country?

A Serbia   C Russia
B Croatia   D France

186 The country of SFR Yugoslavia ceased to exist in what year?

A 1990   C 1994
B 1992   D 1996

187 South Sudan gained independence from Sudan in what year?

A 1991   C 2006
B 2001   D 2011

188 Tonga is a small island nation in which continent?

A Asia   C Australia & Oceania
B Africa   D North America

189 Sao Tome and Principe is a small island nation in which continent?

A Asia   C Australia & Oceania
B Africa   D North America

190 Dominica is a small island nation in which continent?

A Asia   C Australia & Oceania
B Africa   D North America

191 **Leningrad is the former name of what modern city?**
A Rostov On Don
B Moscow
C Volgograd
D St. Petersburg

192 **Stalingrad is the former name of what modern city?**
A Rostov On Don
B Moscow
C Volgograd
D St. Petersburg

193 **Who was the last leader of the Soviet Union before it's collapse?**
A Boris Yeltsin
B Mikhael Gorbachev
C Vladimir Putin
D Gennady Yanayev

194 **Which currency is used in most West African countries?**
A Franc
B Dirham
C Dollar
D Leone

195 **Rosa Parks famously refused to give up her seat on a bus in which U.S. town?**
A Birmingham
B Baton Rouge
C Montgomery
D Mobile

196 **What is the Italian name for Switzerland?**
A Svizra
B Suissia
C Swizzerlano
D Svizzera

197 **What is the German name for France?**
A Franckland
B Francien
C Frankreich
D France

198 **What is the French name for the United States?**
A Americie-Unis
B Etats-Unis
C Unie Etats
D Unie D'Etat

199 **Saxony is a region of which country?**
A Denmark
B Norway
C Poland
D Germany

200 **What is the capital of the self-declared republic of Somaliland?**
A Galkayo
B Mogadishu
C Hargeisa
D Bosaso

201 Socotra is an island in the Arabian Sea belonging to which country?

A Oman
B Yemen
C United Kingdom
D Somalia

202 Socotra is an island belonging to which continent?

A Africa
B Australia & Oceania
C Asia
D Europe

203 The Midian mountains is a mountain range in which country?

A Saudi Arabia
B Yemen
C Oman
D Ethiopia

204 Which African country has the highest altitude capital city?

A Kenya
B Burundi
C Lesotho
D Uganda

205 The Great Escarpment is a topological feature of mainly which country?

A Brazil
B Australia
C United States
D South Africa

206 Which country was formerly called Abyssinia?

A Armenia
B Iraq
C Ethiopia
D Morocco

207 The Chernobyl Disaster in 1984 occurred in which modern day country?

A Belarus
B Ukraine
C Russia
D Kazakhstan

208 What is the capital of Mozambique?

A Maputo
B Bulawayo
C Nacala
D Mbabane

209 The Grand Canyon is in which U.S. state?

A Nevada
B California
C Arizona
D New Mexico

210 How many Canadian provinces and territories are landlocked?

A 0
B 1
C 2
D 3

211 Chichen Itza, the site of a major Inca city, is located in which modern day Mexican state?

A Campeche   **C** Tabasco
B Quintana Roo   **D** Yutacan

212 To the nearest 100 metres/feet, how tall is the CN tower in Toronto?

A 900 feet, 300 metres   **C** 1500 feet, 500 metres
B 1200 feet, 400 metres   **D** 1800 feet, 600 metres

213 Which continent is the only one to lie in all four hemispheres?

A Australia & Oceania   **C** Asia
B North America   **D** South America

214 The Detroit metropolitan area also extends to which Canadian city?

A Mississauga   **C** Windsor
B London   **D** Hamilton

215 What is the largest Mexican state?

A Sonora   **C** Coahuila
B Chihuahua   **D** Durango

216 How many countries does the equator pass through?

A 4   **C** 10
B 7   **D** 13

217 What F is the name of Berlin's TV tower in Alexanderplatz?

A Berliner TV Tower   **C** Fernsehrturm
B Deutschland TV Tower   **D** Alexander TV Tower

218 What is the largest city within Crimea?

A Krasnodar   **C** Odessa
B Sevastopol   **D** Samsun

219 Hispaniola is an island comprised of what 2 countries?

A Dominica & Dominican Republic   **C** Dominica & Haiti
B Haiti & Dominican Republic   **D** Cuba & Haiti

220 What is the only sea without any coasts?

A Sargasso Sea   **C** Bermuda Sea
B Laccadive Sea   **D** Labrador Sea

/20

221 If one sailed from the Philippines to Vietnam, what body of water does one cross?

A Yellow Sea

B Philippine Sea

C South China Sea

D Celebes Sea

222 The Laccadive Sea is found in which ocean?

A Atlantic Ocean

B Indian Ocean

C Pacific Ocean

D Southern Ocean

223 On what island is the westernmost point of the U.S?

A Andreanof Island

B St. Lawrence Island

C Diomede Island

D Attu Island

224 What is the distance between Key West in Florida and Cuba?

A 60 miles

B 90 miles

C 120 miles

D 150 miles

225 The Bering Strait divides which 2 oceans?

A Arctic and Pacific Ocean

B Atlantic and Pacific Ocean

C Arctic and Atlantic Ocean

D Indian and Pacific Ocean

226 If you traveled along the Earth's surface, what is the shortest distance between the North Pole and the South Pole?

A 24,310 miles

B 14,023 miles

C 12,430 miles

D 21,430 miles

227 What is the capital of Paraguay?

A Asuncion

B Cordoba

C Santa Cruz

D Mendosa

228 The Wakhan Corridor is a panhandle belonging to which country?

A Pakistan

B Nepal

C Tajikistan

D Afghanistan

229 The Pamir mountains lies mostly in which country?

A Kyrgyzstan

B China

C Pakistan

D Tajikistan

230 The Abraj Al Bait is a complex of buildings, located in which city?

A Medina

B Amman

C Mecca

D Riyadh

231 Pangaea was a super-continent that first split into which 2 continents?

A Rodinia & Gondwanaland
B Pannotia & Laurasia
C Laurasia & Gondwanaland
D Rodinia & Laurasia

232 Which latitude provides a border for the Southern (Antarctic) ocean?

A 50th parallel south
B 55th parallel south
C 60th parallel south
D Antarctic Circle

233 The historic Turkish city of Adrianapole is now called?

A Edirne
B Antalya
C Mersin
D Bursa

234 Which island is home to the most countries?

A Hispaniola
B Ireland
C Timor
D Borneo

235 The city of Sopron, originally an Austrian city, is now part of which country?

A Germany
B Hungary
C Switzerland
D Czech Republic

236 What is the name of Turkey's largest island?

A Bozcaada
B Lesvos
C Gokkceada
D Uzun Ada

237 Bethlehem is a biblical town located in which modern country?

A Palestine
B Lebanon
C Israel
D Syria

238 The gulf that connects Israel to the Red Sea is called what?

A Gulf of Israel
B Gulf of Suez
C Gulf Of Aqaba/Eilat
D Gulf Of Aden

239 What is the second longest river in Africa?

A Gambezi River
B Congo River
C Niger River
D White Nile River

240 Wilno, the name for the Polish city until 1939, is now the capital of which country?

A Belarus
B Lithuania
C Poland
D Slovakia

/20

241 What is the name of the Underground train service in Berlin?

A U-Bahn

B Metro

C Underground

D S-Bahn

242 Al-Gharb is the Arabic name and the origin of the name of which European region?

A Albania

B Alps

C Alicante

D Algarve

243 Bohemia is a traditional region of which modern day country?

A Slovakia

B Czech Republic

C Germany

D Austria

244 Located on the Azores, what is the highest mountain of Portugal?

A Pica Neblina

B Monte Pico

C Monte Rosa

D Pica Rescordia

245 A lusophone is someone who speaks which language?

A Spanish

B Greek

C Portuguese

D Turkish

246 The hammer and compass was an emblem displayed on which European flag until 1990?

A Romania

B Bulgaria

C Soviet Union

D East Germany

247 What is both a Chinese island and the southernmost prefecture of China?

A Hainan

B Macau

C Guangdong

D Spratly Islands

248 What is the southernmost subject (region) of Russia?

A Chechnya

B Krasnodar Krai

C Dagestan

D Astrakhan

249 The southernmost point of the Soviet Union is closer to the equator than how many African capitals?

A 0

B 1

C 2

D 3

250 What river flows through Baghdad?

A Zab

B Mesopotamia

C Tigris

D Hammar

251 What percentage of the River Nile is found in Egypt?
A 13%
B 22%
C 37%
D 53%

252 Which city from the list below is closest to the equator?
A Kingston, Jamaica
B Bangalore, India
C Bangkok, Thailand
D Darwin, Australia

253 Which U.S. state has the most active volcanoes?
A Alaska
B California
C Washington
D Hawaii

254 Which country has the largest EEZ (Exclusive Economic Zone)?
A France
B United Kingdom
C Indonesia
D Canada

255 Arunachal Pradesh is a disputed territory between India and which other country?
A Pakistan
B Nepal
C Bangladesh
D China

256 What was the majority indigenous population of the Caribbean known as?
A Kalinagos
B Tainos
C Island Caribs
D Guanahatabey

257 Which city from the list below is closest to the North Pole?
A Oslo
B St. Petersburg
C Helsinki
D Stockholm

258 How many countries does the Arctic Circle pass through?
A 2
B 4
C 6
D 8

259 From the answers below, which is the largest island?
A Honshu
B Great Britain
C South Island
D Java

260 Which city does Sheremetyevo International Airport serve?
A Almaty
B Kiev
C Moscow
D St. Petersburg

261 O'Hare International airport in 2020, has the most runways for any airport, with how many runways?
A 6
B 8
C 10
D 12

262 The land area of Russia is what integer percentage of the total land area?
A 4%
B 8%
C 12%
D 16%

263 The land area of South America is what integer percentage of the total land area?
A 4%
B 8%
C 12%
D 16%

264 How many countries in the world officially use the Fahrenheit temperature system?
A 1
B 3
C 5
D 7

265 What is the largest island in the Mediterranean Sea?
A Sardinia
B Crete
C Sicily
D Mallorca

266 What is the IATA Airport Code for Tehran's Imam Khomeini International Airport?
A TKA
B IKA
C THA
D TIK

267 What is the name of the largest city on the island of Tahiti?
A Funafuti
B Papeete
C Uturoa
D Tiputa

268 What is the name of the largest island of Hawaii state?
A Maui
B Kauai
C O'ahu
D Hawai'i

269 How many countries border Germany?
A 5
B 7
C 9
D 11

270 How long was the Berlin Wall to the nearest 10 miles?
A 50 miles
B 100 miles
C 150 miles
D 200 miles

271 Copenhagen, the capital of Denmark, sits on what island?

A Zealand
B Gotland
C Fyn
D Lolland

272 The Aland Islands are an autonomous region belonging mainly to which country?

A Sweden
B Estonia
C Finland
D Denmark

273 Which two mountain ranges are widely accepted as the boundary between Europe and Asia in Russia?

A Caucasus Mountains
B Atlas Mountains
C Ural Mountains
D Alps

274 How many Canadian provinces have land more southerly than the 49th parallel?

A 5
B 7
C 9
D 11

275 The 38th parallel was provisionally used to determine the border of which 2 countries after WW2?

A South and North Korea
B South and North Vietnam
C South and North Yemen
D Austria and Czech Republic

276 What is Canada's largest island?

A Ellesmere Island
B Victoria Island
C Baffin Island
D Newfoundland

277 What is Russia's largest island?

A October Revolution Island
B Bolshevik Island
C Severny Island
D Sakhalin

278 What is the largest glacier in the world?

A Siachen Glacier
B Lambert-Fisher glacier
C Fox Glacier
D Fedchenko Glacier

279 What is the largest settlement on the remote Kerguelen Islands?

A Port Denis
B Port Jeanne D'Arc
C Port-Aux-Francais
D Port Noumea

280 What parallel is used to describe Antarctica in the Antarctic treaty?

A 50th parallel south
B 55th parallel south
C 60th parallel south
D Antractica Circle

281 **What is the name of the U.S. research station on the South Pole?**

A Amundsen Station
B Washington Station
C Amundsen-Scott Station
D Scott Station

282 **Jan Mayen is an island belonging to which country?**

A Iceland
B Norway
C Denmark
D Canada

283 **Before the U.S. purchase of the U.S Virgin Islands, which country did they belong to?**

A Sweden
B France
C Netherlands
D Denmark

284 **Charles De Gaulle was the first president of the French Fifth republic, formed in which year?**

A 1945
B 1948
C 1955
D 1958

285 **Swahili is an official language in how many countries?**

A 2
B 4
C 6
D 8

286 **Jubaland (also Jubbaland) is a state in which African country?**

A Somalia
B Nigeria
C Sudan
D South Africa

287 **What is the only autonomous federal subject (region) of Russia?**

A Siberian Autonomous Oblast
B Kamchatka Autonomous Oblast
C Chechnya Autonomous Oblast
D Jewish Autonomous Oblast

288 **What French city lies closest to the border with Germany?**

A Nancy
B Strasbourg
C Mulhouse
D Metz

289 **North Asia is also often refered to as?**

A Siberia
B Russia
C Kamchatka
D Arctic Asia

290 **The city of Las Vegas is found in which desert?**

A Sonora Desert
B Mojave Desert
C Chihuahuan Desert
D Great Basin

291 **As well as Nunavut, what are the other 2 Canadian territories?**

A Northwest & Newfoundland   **C** Yukon & Northwest
B Northwest & Saskatchewan   **D** Yukon & Newfoundland

292 **What is the largest Australian territory (not state)?**

A Queensland   **C** Western Australia
B Northern   **D** Victoria

293 **The Australian Christmas Islands is the closest to which Indonesian island?**

A Bali   **C** New Guinea
B Sumatra   **D** Java

294 **What is the largest country to not have it's own airport?**

A Liechtenstein   **C** Barbados
B Luxembourg   **D** Andorra

295 **The coat of arms of which European Union country bear the hammer and sickle?**

A Romania   **C** Italy
B Austria   **D** Slovenia

296 **The 10 highest waterfalls in Europe are located in which country?**

A Slovakia   **C** Norway
B Switzerland   **D** France

297 **The 'Big Easy' is a nickname for which U.S. city?**

A New Orleans   **C** Miami
B Orlando   **D** Chicago

298 **Triglav is the highest mountain of which country?**

A Slovakia   **C** Slovenia
B Serbia   **D** Albania

299 **Which Scottish county is home to the most native Scottish Gaelic speakers?**

A Aberdeenshire   **C** Highland
B Outer Hebrides   **D** Dumfries & Galloway

300 **Potola Palace may be found in which Tibetian city?**

A Lhasa   **C** Shigatse
B Thimphu   **D** Tingri

301 Which river flows through St. Petersburg?
A River Don
C Volkhov River
B River Volga
D Neva River

302 A European car with the letter E on the number plate denotes that the car is from which country?
A Estonia
C Spain
B Egypt
D Switzerland

303 Marco Polo airport is located by which city?
A Trieste
C Rome
B Naples
D Venice

304 Italian unification occured in which decade?
A 1800s
C 1840s
B 1820s
D 1860s

305 The Hoggar mountains are located in which country?
A Kenya
C Iran
B Algeria
D Sudan

306 What is the southernmost Greek island?
A Crete
C Rhodes
B Chrisi
D Gavdos

307 Inner Mongolia is the name of a region in which country?
A Mongolia
C China
B Kazakhstan
D Russia

308 West Azerbaijan and East Azerbaijan are provinces belonging to which country?
A Armenia
C Iran
B Azerbaijan
D Russia

309 What is the name of the Azerbaijani exclave bordering Armenia and Iran?
A Nakhchivan
C Nagorno-Karabakh
B Artsakh
D Abkhazia

310 What is the name of Croatia in Croatian?
A Croazia
C Magyavatska
B Hrvatska
D Shqivatska

311 **What is the name of Albania in Albanian?**
A Al-Banha   C Magyaperia
B Hrqperia   D Shqiperia

312 **What is the name of Hungary in Hungarian?**
A Hungarien   C Magyarország
B Hryarország   D Shqiyarország

313 **Mount Stanley, at 5109m, is the highest peak of which African mountain range?**
A Ruwenzori   C Sami Mountains
B Eastern Rift Mountains D Simien Mountains

314 **Which hemisphere, from Northern or Southern, does Kenya have more territory in?**

315 **How many countries border the Black Sea?**
A 3   C 5
B 4   D 6

316 **The gulf of Finland separates which 2 capital cities?**
A Stockholm & Tallinn   C Helsinki & Stockholm
B Helsinki & Tallinn   D Tallinn & Moscow

317 **The Tatra Mountains are used as a natural border for which 2 countries?**
A Uzbekistan & Kazakhstan C Poland & Slovakia
B Guatemala & Belize   D Croatia & Bosnia & Herzegovina

318 **Which one of the U.S. cities below is the closest to Canada?**
A Seattle   C Cleveland
B Milwaukee   D Minneapolis

319 **The panhandle in Namibia is known as?**
A Caprivi Panhandle   C Caprivi Corridor
B Caprivi Narrows   D Caprivi Strip

320 **What is the name of the state found in both India and Pakistan?**
A Rajahstan   C Punjab
B Sindh   D Gujarat

321 Along with France and Finland, what is the only other country to begin with F?

322 Mountains with over 1500 metres of prominence are known as?

A Very Prominent Mountains   **C** Ultra Prominent Mountains
B Super Prominent Mountains   **D** Highly Prominent Mountains

323 What is the Rapa Nui more commonly known as?

A The native people of Tahiti   **C** The native people of Polynesia
B The native people of Hawaii   **D** The native people of Easter Island

324 Along with Micronesia and Polynesia, what other region forms Oceania?

A Melanesia   **C** Mononesia
B Macronesia   **D** Indonesia

325 Hawaii belongs to which region of Oceania?

A Micronesia   **C** Mononesia
B Polynesia   **D** Macronesia

326 The Niagara falls occurs between which 2 of the Great Lakes?

A Lake Superior & Huron   **C** Lake Huron & Erie
B Lake Michigan & Huron   **D** Lake Erie & Ontario

327 The most northerly point of the contiguous United States is known as the Northwest Angle, and may be found in which state?

A Washington   **C** Michigan
B Minnesota   **D** Wisconsin

328 Which country, in the UTC+14 time zone, will be the first place to celebrate New Years?

A Fiji   **C** Kiribati
B Tonga   **D** Marshall Islands

329 Matthew Flinders popularised the name of which modern day commonwealth country?

A India   **C** Canada
B Australia   **D** Kenya

330 Which U.S. state has the largest proportion of Hispanics/Latinos amongst their population?

A Texas   **C** Arizona
B New Mexico   **D** California

331 **French is the official language of how many Canadian provinces?**
A 1   C 3
B 2   D 4

332 **Before the Burj Khalifa, what was the previous tallest building in the world?**
A CN Tower   C Taipei 101
B Shanghai Tower   D One World Trade Center

333 **Lugano in Switzerland sits on which lake?**
A Lake Lugano   C Lake Maggiore
B Lake Ticino   D Lake Como

334 **Piedmont is a region of which country?**
A France   C Monaco
B Switzerland   D Italy

335 **The Republic of Venice was a historic country that lost it's independence in what decade?**
A 1790s   C 1860s
B 1810s   D 1910s

336 **To the nearest mile, what is the distance between the southern tip of Spain and Morocco?**
A 6 miles   C 18 miles
B 9 miles   D 36 miles

337 **Santiago de Compostella is the capital of which Spanish province?**
A Aragon   C Galicia
B Cantabria   D Catalonia

338 **As of 2020, which one of the largest French speaking countries in the world is not part of La Francophonie?**
A Cote D'Ivoire   C Democratic Republic of Congo
B Algeria   D Canada

339 **What is the largest Canadian island lying in the Pacific Ocean?**
A Victoria Island   C Haida Gwaii
B Graham Island   D Vancouver Island

340 **South Sakhalin was once a Japanese possession, the Russian border of which located on which parallel?**
A 43rd parallel   C 48th parallel
B 45th parallel   D 50th parallel

/20

341 **To travel by land from the most northern point of Africa in Tunisia, to the most southern in South Africa, what is the minimum amount of countries you would need to pass?**

A 6   C 8
B 7   D 9

342 **Brazil shares a border with all but which 2 South American countries?**

A Uruguay   C Colombia
B Ecuador   D Chile

343 **Cappadocia is a large plateau in which country?**

A Lebanon   C Italy
B Greece   D Turkey

344 **What is the largest religious structure in the world (as of 2020)?**

A Potala Palace   C Angkor Wat
B St. Peter's Basilica   D Imam Ali Mosque

345 **Merlion, a half lion, half fish imaginary creature, is the mascot of which island nation?**

A Indonesia   C Hong Kong
B Singapore   D Taiwan

346 **The NATO headquarters are located in which city?**

A Washington D.C.   C Brussels
B New York   D Luxembourg City

347 **Mainland Denmark basically encompasses which peninsula?**

A Gotland   C Schleswig
B Jutland   D Smaland

348 **Tiraspol is the capital of which self-declared republic?**

A Luhansk Republic   C Donetsk Republic
B Transnistria   D South Ossetia

349 **What is the main spoken language in Eswatini?**

A Siswati   C Swahili
B Bantu   D Swazi

350 **Martinique is a Caribbean island and located between 2 independent island countries, Dominica to the north and what country to the south?**

A St. Vincent & The Grenadines   C St. Lucia
B Grenada   D Antigua & Barbuda

351 The gulf of Paria lies between Venezuela and which
other country?
A Trinidad and Tobago   C Barbados
B Jamaica   D Colombia

352 What is the alphabet (script) used by the Austronesian
languages?
A Chinese Alphabet   C Khmer Script
B Latin Alphabet   D Thai Script

353 What is the only continental African country to have
it's capital on an island?
A Equatorial Guinea   C Gabon
B Cape Verde   D Madagascar

354 If the official name for France is the French Republic,
what is the official name for Mexico?
A Socialist Republic of Mexico   C United Mexican States
B Federal Republic of Mexico   D Mexican Republic

355 How many countries as of 2020 retain an official
ideaology of Marxism-Leninism?
A 0   C 4
B 2   D 6

356 Having lost it's sovereignty in 1492, what was the last
Islamic Emirate in Spain?
A Emirate of Grenada   C Emirate of Sevilla
B Emirate of Cordoba   D Emirate of Andalusia

357 Often marked as the end of the British empire, when
was Hong Kong returned to Chinese rule?
A 1975   C 1997
B 1992   D 2000

358 How many Canadian provinces and territories border
the Hudson Bay?
A 2   C 4
B 3   D 5

359 The centre of Kansas City is located in which U.S.
state?
A Nebraska   C Kansas
B Missouri   D Oklahoma

360 The U.S. state of Tennessee borders how many other
U.S. states?
A 4   C 7
B 6   D 8

361 A tundra climate in the Koppen classification is one officially defined as no month exceeding an average of what temperature?

A 0°C (32°F)

B 5°C (41°F)

C 10°C (50°F)

D 12°C (53.6°F)

362 How many countries are completed surrounded by another country?

A 1

B 2

C 3

D 4

363 Which from the list below is the longest bi-national border?

A China - Mongolia

B Norway - Sweden

C Argentina - Chile

D Kazakhstan - Russia

364 True or false, the island of Mauritius is larger than the neighboring island of Reunion?

365 What is the name of the most easterly state of Mexico, and home to the popular tourist city of Cancun?

A Chiapas

B Quintana Roo

C Yutacan

D Oaxaca

366 Which country is the largest producer of Soybean?

A USA (United States)

B Brazil

C China

D Indonesia

367 New Zealand is named after a province in which country?

A Netherlands

B United Kingdom

C Denmark

D Spain

368 How many countries have a capital of the same name?

A 5

B 7

C 9

D 11

369 A tropical climate in the Koppen classification is one officially defined as no month dropping below an average of what temperature?

A 10°C (50°F)

B 18°C (64.4°F)

C 20°C (68°F)

D 22°C (71.6°F)

370 Which religion has the 3rd largest amount of followers?

A Islam

B Buddhism

C Christianity

D Hinduism

371 Helvetia is the Latin name for which country?
A Austria
B Italy
C France
D Switzerland

372 Bermuda is closest to which U.S. state?
A New Jersey
B North Carolina
C South Carolina
D Florida

373 The U.S state of Michigan borders how many of the 5 Great Lakes?
A 1
B 2
C 3
D 4

374 What is the capital of Xinjiang, the largest perfecture of China?
A Urumqi
B Chengdu
C Xi'an
D Kashgar

375 What is the southernmost island of Italy?
A Pantelleria
B Sicily
C Lampedusa
D Sharqi Island

376 Praia, the capital of Cape Verde is closest to which mainland African country?
A Morocco
B Sierra Leone
C Senegal
D Mauritania

377 Which oceanic current brings a year round mild climate to coastal Namibia?
A Antarctic Current
B Benguela Current
C Canary Current
D South Africa Current

378 The Tivoli Gardens are located in which city?
A The Hague
B Hamburg
C Stockholm
D Copenhagen

379 How many stars are there on the flag of the European Union?
A 10
B 12
C 16
D 24

380 The island of Maluku belongs to which country?
A Tanzania
B Indonesia
C Papua New Guinea
D Madagascar

381 Mosquito Coast is located in which country?

A Nicaragua   C Panama
B Costa Rica   D El Salvador

382 Motown is another name for which U.S. city?

A Cincinnati   C Detroit
B Cleveland   D Chicago

383 Which 2 U.S. states are rectangular?

A Utah & Wyoming   C Colorado & Wyoming
B New Mexico & Wyoming   D Arizona & Wyoming

384 What is the largest city within the Irish county of Leinster?

A Dublin   C Limerick
B Galway   D Cork

385 Switzerland is unique for it's policy of privacy in which profession?

A Law   C Banking
B Medicine   D Religion

386 Nihongo is the endonym for which language?

A Mandarin Chinese   C Korean
B Japanese   D Vietnamese

387 What island is the most populous in the world?

A Honshu   C Borneo
B Great Britain   D Java

388 What is the largest island of The Philippines?

A Palawan   C Panay
B Luzon   D Mindanao

389 Which African capital is named after an American president?

A Niamey   C Monrovia
B N'Djamena   D Lome

390 Part of the Great Rift Valley is submerged under what sea?

A Arabian Sea   C Caribbean Sea
B Mediterranean Sea   D Red Sea

391 The Arc De Triomphe in Paris has how many avenues leading to it?

A 8   **C** 12
B 10   **D** 16

392 What was the name of the territory set aside for Black people during South Africa's apartheid era?

A Boerstan   **C** Bantustan
B S.A.N. reservations   **D** Lesotho

393 Mandalay is the second-biggest city of which country?

A Myanmar   **C** Vietnam
B Thailand   **D** Singapore

394 The Singapore Strait separates Singapore from which group of islands belonging to Indonesia?

A Spratly Islands   **C** Riau Islands
B Visayas   **D** Banda Arc

395 What is the name of the town at the northern tip of Ellesmere Island, and the most northerly permanently inhabited place in the world?

A Alert   **C** Utqiagvik
B Longyearbyen   **D** Eureka

396 Without counting dependencies and self governing territories, how many countries have a border with only one other country?

A 7   **C** 21
B 14   **D** 33

397 Heligoland, an island that once owned by the UK, is now part of which country?

A Norway   **C** Denmark
B Kenya   **D** Germany

398 What is the German name for the city of Munich?

A Munichen   **C** Munster
B Munchen   **D** Munerich

399 What was the Italian name for the now Croatian city of Dubrovnik?

A Spalato   **C** Adriatica
B Dolmatio   **D** Ragusa

400 Zakynthos is the local name for which popular Greek tourist destination?

A Malia   **C** Corfu
B Zante   **D** Rhodes

401 **The Corinth Canal separates the Greek mainland from which peninsula?**
   A Peloponnesse   **C** Dodecanese
   B Balkan   **D** Palatennesse

402 **What is the highest volcano in Europe?**
   A Mt. Etna   **C** Mt. Elbrus
   B Mt. Vesuvius   **D** Teide

403 **Which European country has the largest amount of active volcanoes (as of 2020)?**
   A Italy   **C** Greece
   B Cyprus   **D** Iceland

404 **What is the largest national forest in the USA?**
   A Tongass   **C** Samon-Challis
   B Yellowstone   **D** Humboldt-Toiyabe

405 **What strait connects the Red Sea to the Arabian Sea?**
   A Straits of Tiran   **C** Strait of Hormuz
   B Beb-El-Mandeb   **D** Abdul-El-Sharm

406 **Belgium's capital, Brussels, is located in which Belgian region?**
   A Brussels   **C** Capital
   B Wallonia   **D** Flanders

407 **What is the Westernmost island of Greece?**
   A Othonoi   **C** Kastellerizo
   B Corfu   **D** kos

408 **The Sea of Azov is strictly speaking in what ocean?**
   A Indian Ocean   **C** Pacific Ocean
   B Arctic Ocean   **D** Atlantic Ocean

409 **The remains of the Aral Sea falls between which 2 countries?**
   A Kazakhstan & Turkmenistan   **C** Kazakhstan & Russia
   B Kazakhstan & Uzbekistan   **D** Kazakhstan & Kyrgyzstan

410 **Whilst Morocco administers the majority of Western Sahara (as of 2020), which other state administers the remaining part?**
   A Mauritania   **C** SADR (Sahrawi Arab Democratic Rep.)
   B Algeria   **D** United Nations

411 Which U.S. state would you be in if you crossed the Mississippi River from Memphis, Tennessee?

A Kentucky   C Louisiana
B Missouri   D Arkansas

412 Sioux City, located in the U.S. state of Iowa, is only a river crossing away from which 2 other U.S. states?

A Nebraska & South Dakota   C Missouri & Illinois
B Minnesota & South Dakota   D Wisconsin & Illinois

413 Of the 8 countries the Prime meridian passes through, how many of these countries do not observe GMT (Greenwich Meridian Time)?

A 0   C 2
B 1   D 3

414 How many time zones are found in Africa?

A 4   C 6
B 5   D 7

415 What island nation may be found in the Mozambique Channel?

A Maldives   C Mauritius
B Seychelles   D Comoros

416 Mafia Island is a part of which country?

A Tanzania   C Italy
B Cuba   D Albania

417 Which state is the southernmost tip of India located in?

A Maharashtra   C Tamil Nadu
B Kerala   D Puducherry

418 Which country has the smallest coast line in the Persian Gulf (Arabian Gulf)?

A Kuwait   C Bahrain
B Iraq   D Qatar

419 Romansh is an official language of which country?

A Romania   C Switzerland
B Russia   D France

420 By population, what is Iran's 2nd largest city after Tehran?

A Mashhad   C Karachi
B Erbil   D Isfahan

421 Often incorrectly listed as Yaren, which island nation does not officially have a capital city?
A Tuvalu
B Vanuatu
C Nauru
D Marshall Islands

422 How many sovereign country flags are only red and white?
A 5
B 11
C 16
D 25

423 Which country has land closest to the North pole?
A Russia
B Canada
C Norway
D Greenland (Denmark)

424 Which country from those listed below is closest to the North Pole?
A Ireland
B Lithuania
C Mongolia
D Contiguous U.S.A

425 Which river, flowing into the Congo River, does Central African Republic's capital, Bangui, lie on?
A Mbomou
B Gambezi
C Ubangi
D Sangha

426 Which land from those listed below is closest to the Equator?
A Finland
B Iceland
C Greenland
D Norway

427 What is the largest desert in the Americas?
A Atacama Desert
B Patagonian Desert
C Sonora Desert
D Great Basin

428 Which is the only country to exhibit every major climatic zone?
A Russia
B India
C USA
D China

429 Tribhuvan International airport is closest to which Asian capital?
A Kathmandu
B New Delhi
C Thimphu
D Dhaka

430 Between the 6 European microstates, how many countries do they collectively border?
A 4
B 5
C 6
D 7

431 The Kara Sea may be found in which ocean?

A Arctic Ocean   C Atlantic Ocean
B Southern Ocean   D Pacific Ocean

432 Baarle-Hertog is a city found in an exclave of which country?

A Netherlands   C Belgium
B Germany   D France

433 Harar, often said to be the 4th Holy city of Islam, may be found in which country?

A Iran   C Ethiopia
B India   D Morocco

434 What is the name of the strait that separates the North and South Island of New Zealand?

A Zealand Strait   C Foveaux Strait
B Rakaia Strait   D Cook Strait

435 Mount Nimba is the highest point of which 2 African countries?

A Central African Rep. & DRC   C Kenya & Tanzania
B Cote D'Ivoire & Guinea   D Burkina Faso & Niger

436 The Tuvan People's Republic was a state from 1922–1946 that is now part of which modern day country?

A Russia   C Mongolia
B Kazakhstan   D Tajikistan

437 If one crossed from India to China, what would the difference in Time Zone's be?

A 1 hour   C 2 hours
B 1 and a half hours   D 2 and a half hours

438 Marie Curie named an element after the country she was born in. Which country is it?

A Italy   C France
B Poland   D Prussia

439 To the closest 10%, what percentage of the world population lives in a temperate climate?

A 20%   C 40%
B 30%   D 50%

440 The Rio De La Plata is a river with the capitals of which two countries lying on it?

A Brazil   C Uruguay
B Argentina   D Paraguay

/20

441 Which island is home to over 700 native languages?

A Java
B Sulawesi
C New Guinea
D Honshu

442 What P is the city of Beijing also known as?

A Piongtang
B Pyongyang
C Patek
D Peking

443 The Baltic States is a name to refer collectively to which three countries?

A Lithuania, Latvia and Estonia
B Bulgaria, Romania, Moldova
C Norway, Sweden, Finland
D Slovenia, Slovakia, Serbia

444 What S is the University of Paris more commonly known as?

A Seine
B Saint-Denis
C Sorbonne
D Soleil

445 What is the name of the palace that was home to the French monarchy, before their abdiction?

A Luxembourg Palace
B Versailles Palace
C Sacre Coeur
D Elysee Palace

446 Flowing through London, which city, known for it's university, does the River Thames also flow through?

A Durham
B Buckingham
C Oxford
D Cambridge

447 What U.S. state is home to the literally named town of 'Frostproof'?

A Hawaii
B Texas
C Louisiana
D Florida

448 Which one of these countries is not landlocked?

A Azerbaijan
B Burkina Faso
C Jordan
D Zambia

449 What motorway circles the London built-up area?

A M1
B M6
C M25
D M30

450 What highway connects New York to Miami?

A Interstate 90
B Interstate 66
C Interstate 40
D Interstate 95

451 Bellagio, a famous Las Vegas resort, is also the name of an Italian village that is situated on which lake?

A Lake Garda
B Lake Como
C Lake Constance
D Lake Maggiore

452 Which U.S. state, if measured as an independent country, would have the 8th largest GDP of all countries as of 2020?

A New York State
B California
C Florida
D Texas

453 What two cities does the historic Route 66 connect?

A Los Angeles & New York
B San Francisco & New York
C San Diego & Chicago
D Santa Monica & Chicago

454 Lutetia is the Roman name for which modern day European city?

A Paris
B London
C Lyon
D Madrid

455 Camp Nou is the home stadium of which European football (soccer) team?

A PSG
B Juventus
C FC Barcelona
D Real Madrid

456 In how many countries did Albert Einstein have a citizenship throughout his life?

A 1
B 2
C 4
D 6

457 Highway 401 and Autoroute 20 in Canada connects Windsor to which other Canadian city?

A Montreal
B St. Johns
C Ottawa
D Quebec City

458 The district of Waterloo in London is named after what event in 1815?

A Waterloo Civil War
B Coronation of British King
C Battle Of Waterloo
D Independence of Waterloo

459 Which Central American country is the only one to not border the Atlantic Ocean?

A Belize
B El Salvador
C Guatemala
D Honduras

460 Which structure succeeded the Great Pyramid of Giza as the tallest structure in 1311 AD?

A Canterbury Cathedral
B Notre Dame
C Lincoln Cathedral
D Cologne Cathedral

461 What is the capital of the territory of Greenland?

A Nuuk   C Gotthab
B Oqaatsub   D Nuugaatsiaq

462 Holding the Winter Olympics of 2014, in which country is Sochi located?

A Canada   C Finland
B Norway   D Russia

463 Which U.S. state contains at least part of the 10 largest native American reservations?

A New Mexico   C Arizona
B Oklahoma   D Texas

464 Which Canadian city literally means 'muddy water'?

A Calgary   C Mississisauga
B Winnipeg   D Saskatoon

465 What river flows through Cambridge, UK?

A River Trent   C River Severn
B River Ouse   D River Cam

466 Heathrow Airport is what direction from London City?

A North   C South
B East   D West

467 What Japanese city preceded Tokyo as it's capital?

A Osaka   C Okinawa
B Kyoto   D Sapporo

468 What U.S. state was named after the British Queen Elizabeth I?

A New Hampshire   C Virginia
B Maryland   D Georgia

469 Which Arab nation has the highest proportion of followers of Christianity?

A Syria   C Jordan
B Tunisia   D Lebanon

470 Which U.S. state witnesses the most tornadoes annually?

A Texas   C Arkansas
B Oklahoma   D Missouri

471 Which country has the largest Muslim population in the world (as of 2020)?

A Pakistan   **C** Indonesia
B India   **D** Saudi Arabia

472 Which African country has it's flag modelled from the U.S's and is named after the latin word for 'free'?

A Benin   **C** Sierra Leone
B Liberia   **D** Ghana

473 What is Ayer's Rock in Australia also known as?

A Wollongongong   **C** Uluru
B Boolongoo   **D** Alara

474 Which desert may be found in Namibia, Botswana and South Africa?

A Kalahari   **C** Sahel
B Gobi   **D** Namib

475 Which Arab country's national dish is known as 'Fool'?

A Algeria   **C** Egypt
B United Arab Emirates   **D** Saudi Arabia

476 What is the name of the highest mountain in the Atlas Mountains?

A Toubkal   **C** M'Goun
B Jbel Jamhari   **D** Jbel Bou Mecel

477 The Dolomites are a mountain range located in which country?

A United States   **C** Tanzania
B Italy   **D** Australia

478 Which country's high point is the highest?

A Andorra   **C** Australia
B Bulgaria   **D** Brazil

479 The Hida Mountain Range may be found in which country?

A Spain   **C** New Zealand
B United States   **D** Japan

480 The U.S.-Mexican border follows in part which river?

A Colorado River   **C** Yuma River
B The Rio Grande   **D** The El Paso River

/20

481 To the nearest 1000, how many islands belong to Japan?

A 3000   C 7000
B 5000   D 10000

482 Jeju, a popular tourist destination, is an island belonging to which country?

A Vietnam   C Japan
B Thailand   D South Korea

483 What is the name of the highest mountain of South korea?

A Chiri-San   C Halla-San
B Paektu-San   D Bukhan-San

484 Mt. Logan, the highest point of Canada, is how tall?

A 5862m (19,232 feet)   C 6009m (19,715 feet)
B 5959m (19,551 feet)   D 6110m (20,047 feet)

485 What body of water is around nine times saltier than typical ocean water?

A Red Sea   C Caspian Sea
B Dead Sea   D Persian Gulf (Arabian Gulf)

486 The Nazca tectonic plate is an oceanic plate found in which ocean?

A Southern Ocean   C Atlantic Ocean
B Pacific Ocean   D Indian Ocean

487 Which European territory is located in whole on the African plate?

A Sicily   C Cyprus
B Crete   D Malta

488 Savoy is a region of which country?

A Germany   C France
B Italy   D Switzerland

489 Lake Balkhash, one of the largest lakes in Asia, may be found in which country?

A Kazakhstan   C Russia
B Uzbekistan   D Mongolia

490 The Eiger and Matterhorn are emblematic Alpine mountains in which country?

A Austria   C Switzerland
B France   D Italy

491 The American football team known as the 'Steelers' are from which town?

A Cincinnati   C Baltimore
B Pittsburgh   D Rochester

492 The Heat are a basketball team based in which U.S. city?

A New Orleans   C Miami
B Philadelphia   D Dallas

493 Which country hosted the 2002 FIFA world cup?

A United Kingdom   C Germany
B Russia   D Japan

494 Ice Hockey is the official national winter sport of which country?

A Belarus   C Canada
B The Netherlands   D Norway

495 Standard Liege is a football team from which country?

A Belgium   C France
B The Netherlands   D Switzerland

496 Which country is also known as 'White Russia' in many European countries?

A Estonia   C Ukraine
B Belarus   D Mongolia

497 The Ukrainian flag consists of which two colors?

A Red and White   C Red and Blue
B Blue and Yellow   D Red, Yellow, Blue

498 The Australian 'Billabong' is another word for which geographical feature?

A Outcrops   C Lagoon
B Estuary   D Oxbow Lake

499 What is the capital of the European microstate, Liechtenstein?

A Chur   C Vaduz
B Bern   D Innsbruck

500 The Ravens are an American Football team located in which city?

A Cleveland   C Detroit
B Baltimore   D Boston

/20

501 Which city is home to the busiest stock exchange?

A Amsterdam
B New York
C London
D Tokyo

502 Saudi Aramco is a state-owned company, specialising in the sale of what?

A Precious Metals
B Pharmaceuticals
C Petroleum Oil
D Real Estate Services

503 Nantucket is the name of a town, island and county in which U.S. state?

A Connecticut
B Massachusetts
C Rhode Island
D New York State

504 What is the demonym for someone living in Wyoming?

A Wyomingite
B Wyomingian
C Equality Stater
D Wyomish

505 What is the name of Japan's northernmost prefecture?

A Hokkaido
B Wakkanai
C Namuro
D Hakodate

506 What is the name of the city that sits at the mouth of China's longest river, the Yangtze?

A Guangzhou
B Macau
C Beijing
D Shanghai

507 Which Chinese city literally means 'fragrant harbor'?

A Dalian
B Macau
C Hong Kong
D Quanzhou

508 What T is the name of country where you can find the Badakhshan national Park?

A Iran
B Afghanistan
C China
D Tajikistan

509 Which city was the capital of the Spanish Empire in the New World until the 1800s?

A Mexico City
B Lima
C Bogota
D La Paz

510 Which ocean current is credited to mild conditions in South America's Pacific coastline and the extreme aridity of the Atacama desert?

A La Nina Current
B The Humboldt current
C South Pacific Current
D Galapagos Current

511 **What is the mountain range where the highest point of Ethiopia is?**

A Aberdare Mountains   **C** The Semien Mountains
B Bale Mountains   **D** Gambella Mountains

512 **Which African country has the longest coastline?**

A Madagascar   **C** Somalia
B South Africa   **D** Egypt

513 **Which city literally translates to 'The city of Islam'?**

A Riyadh   **C** Abu Dhabi
B Mecca   **D** Islamabad

514 **What is the capital of Nova Scotia?**

A St. Johns   **C** Halifax
B Dartmouth   **D** Yarmouth

515 **The Dalmatian dog is named after the historical region of Dalmatia, now in which present-day country?**

A Italy   **C** Croatia
B Austria   **D** Bosnia & Herzegovina

516 **Where does the Romanian language derive from?**

A Germanic Language   **C** Germanic Language
B Romance Language   **D** Uralic Language

517 **Where does the Hungarian language derive from?**

A Germanic Language   **C** Germanic Language
B Romance Language   **D** Uralic Language

518 **Chad's capital N'Djamena sits close to the border with what other African country?**

A Cameroon   **C** Nigeria
B Central African Republic   **D** South Sudan

519 **What is the formal name for China's currency?**

A Rupee   **C** Renminbi
B Yen   **D** Yuan

520 **Keflavik Airport serves which European city?**

A Tromso   **C** Oslo
B Reykjavik   **D** Bergen

521 New York's first subway system travelled from 145th street to which bridge?
A Manhattan Bridge
B George Washington Bridge
C Williamsburg Bridge
D Brooklyn Bridge

522 Which of the 48 contiguous U.S. state's capital is the southernmost?
A Tampa
B Austin
C Baton Rouge
D Tallahassee

523 If Cuba is the largest island in the Caribbean region, where does Puerto Rico rank?
A 2nd
B 3rd
C 4th
D 5th

524 How many islands have mountains above 4000m?
A 2
B 3
C 4
D 6

525 Which nation is closest to the British Indian Ocean Territory (BIOT)?
A Mauritius
B Sri Lanka
C India (Andaman & Nicobar Islands)
D Maldives

526 What is the southernmost city of New Zealand?
A Christchurch
B Hobart
C Invercargill
D Dunedin

527 Milford Sound is one of the wettest places in the world, being how many times wetter than London?
A 3 times
B 5 times
C 7 times
D 10 times

528 Mt. Rainier, a volcano calculated to erupt in the near future, is located in which U.S. state?
A California
B Washington
C Oregon
D Idaho

529 Which two Hungarian towns facing each other on the River Danube merged in 1872 to form the present-day Hungarian capital?
A Buda and Pest
B Buda and Magyar
C Buda and Danuba
D Buda and Elte

530 Infamous con-man Victor Lustig sold which landmark to a metal dealer for $50,000?
A Big Ben Bell
B Statue of Liberty
C Eiffel Tower
D Golden Gate Bridge

531 Who was the designer of the Statue of Liberty?

A Horace Jones   C Gustave Eiffel
B Frédéric Auguste Bartholdi   D John A. Roebling

532 If one were to rent a 'Rakumi' in Africa, how would one likely be travelling?

A By Horse   C By Camel
B By Donkey   D By Ostrich

533 7-Eleven stores first appeared in which U.S. state?

A Texas   C California
B New York State   D Michigan

534 What T and S are Cuba's top two largest exports?

A Tobacco & Potatoes   C Tobacco & Coffee
B Tobacco & Beans   D Tobacco & Sugar

535 Which of the cities below is closest to the Mexican border?

A Tuscon   C El Paso
B San Diego   D San Antonio

536 'Autostrada' is the local name of the highways of which country?

A Italy   C Portugal
B Spain   D Greece

537 The Italian flag was designed by which French Leader?

A Napoleon III   C Charles De Gaulle
B Adolphe Thiers   D Napoleon Bonaparte

538 Which country's flag features a white dragon?

A Nepal   C Laos
B Bhutan   D Vietnam

539 What is the name of the shade of orange used on the Indian National Flag?

A Mandarin   C Turmeric
B Saffron   D Cumin

540 What feature appears on the national flags of Nordic countries?

A Nordic Coat Of Arms   C Nordic Cross
B Nordic Colors   D Nordic Stripe

/20

541 Which country has the longest school year?
A China
B Japan
C Canada
D Sweden

542 Neuschwanstein Castle is located in which German state?
A Rhineland
B Baden-Württemberg
C Thurinigia
D Bavaria

543 What is Germany's main export product?
A Motor Vehicles
B Machinery
C Pharmaceuticals
D Chemical Goods

544 Northern Norway, Sweden and Finland are inhabited mainly by which people?
A Sapmi
B Eskimo
C Sami
D Samoyed

545 La Scala theater is located in which Italian city?
A Milan
B Naples
C Florence
D Rome

546 Which Italian city is credited for the invention of Pizza?
A Milan
B Naples
C Florence
D Rome

547 What was the capital of West Germany (FRG)?
A Frankfurt
B Koln
C Bonn
D Munich

548 Which country has the largest amount of active volcanoes as of 2020?
A Iceland
B Japan
C Russia
D Indonesia

549 Which Canadian city is closest to U.S. land?
A Toronto
B Montreal
C Vancouver
D Winnipeg

550 Which A is the country where ome may find the city of Ganja?
A Canada
B Nigeria
C United States
D Azerbaijan

551 Which country high points from the list below is the highest?
- **A** Mt. Elbrus, Russia
- **B** Mt. Damavand, Iran
- **C** Mt. Ararat, Turkey
- **D** Pico De Orizaba, Mexico

552 Which country's mainland from the list below is closest to the equator?
- **A** Canada
- **B** Kazakhstan
- **C** France
- **D** Russia

553 To the nearest 1000 miles, what is the distance between New York and Sydney?
- **A** 5000 miles
- **B** 8000 miles
- **C** 10,000 miles
- **D** 12,000 miles

554 To the nearest 1000 miles, what is the distance between New York and Los Angeles?
- **A** 1000 miles
- **B** 2000 miles
- **C** 3000 miles
- **D** 4000 miles

555 What is the IATA airport code for Istanbul airport?
- **A** IST
- **B** ITA
- **C** ISA
- **D** IBA

556 Which U.S. state has the lowest population density?
- **A** Maine
- **B** Vermont
- **C** North Dakota
- **D** Montana

557 Which city is regarded as the birthplace of the Renaissance?
- **A** Milan
- **B** Rome
- **C** Florence
- **D** Paris

558 South Tyrol is a bilingual region of which country?
- **A** Italy
- **B** Austria
- **C** Switzerland
- **D** Slovenia

559 What is the largest lake by surface area in South America?
- **A** Lago Poopo
- **B** Lago Argentino
- **C** Lake Titicaca
- **D** Lago Gral Carrera

560 Which country's mainland comes closest to the equator?
- **A** Spain
- **B** Turkey
- **C** Greece
- **D** New Zealand

/20

561 San Diego's metropolitan area includes which Mexican city?

A Nogales
B Tijuana
C Monterrey
D Ciudad Juarez

562 What is the highest mountain of Laos?

A Phou Bia
B Phnom Aural
C Doi Inthanon
D Fansipan

563 What is the capital of the French overseas territory of New Caledonia?

A Suva
B Koumac
C Noumea
D Apia

564 Which country's mainland from the list below is closest to the equator?

A Saudi Arabia
B Australia
C Chile
D Mexico

565 Which country from the list below is extends further from the equator?

A New Zealand
B Spain
C Japan
D Italy

566 To the nearest 1000 miles, what is the distance between Auckland and London?

A 5000 miles
B 7000 miles
C 9000 miles
D 11,000 miles

567 Which country from the list below is larger?

A Eswatini
B Burundi
C Lesotho
D Rwanda

568 How many chemical elements are named after U.S. states?

A 1
B 2
C 3
D 4

569 True or False, over half of the African countries are larger than the United Kingdom (UK)?

570 Kinshasa in the DRC (Democratic Rep. Of The Congo) is separated from which capital city by the Congo river?

A Bangui
B Juba
C Luanda
D Brazzaville

571 Which country is the world's largest producer of Uranium?

A China   C Russia
B Kazakhstan   D Ukraine

572 The fall of which ancient city in 1453 effectively ended the Roman Empire?

A Lutetia   C Rome
B Constantinople   D Babylon

573 Timbuktu is a city located in which African country?

A Nepal   C India
B Bhutan   D Mali

574 The iconic waterfront known as The Bund is located in what city?

A Hong Kong   C Tokyo
B Singapore   D Shanghai

575 The Carmague wetland in France is an example of what geographic feature?

A River Delta   C Aquifer
B Estuary   D Swamp

576 What is the River that flows through Hamburg in Germany?

A River Danube C River Oder
B River Elbe   D Rhine

577 To the nearest 100 miles, what is the distance between Paris and London?

A 300 miles   C 500 miles
B 400 miles   D 600 miles

578 How many U.S. states are larger than the UK?

A 4   C 11
B 8   D 17

579 What is the most populous country in Africa?

A Egypt   C South Africa
B Nigeria   D Kenya

580 Which city listed below is closest to the equator?

A Miami   C Brisbane
B Dubai   D New Delhi

/20

581 Galdhøpiggen is the highest mountain of which country?

A Norway

B Denmark

C Iceland

D Sweden

582 Which country has the highest population density?

A Singapore

B Bangladesh

C Monaco

D Bahrain

583 Which country is the world's largest producer of Gold?

A Russia

B South Africa

C Sierra Leone

D China

584 Ajax football team is located in which European country?

A Belgium

B Netherlands

C Italy

D Croatia

585 Which London Underground line is colored red?

A Circle Line

B Jubilee Line

C Central Line

D Waterloo Line

586 What is the capital of Tuvalu?

A Funafuti

B Suva

C Port Vila

D Nuku'Alofa

587 Byblos, one of the most ancient cities, is located in which country?

A Greece

B Lebanon

C Italy

D Egypt

588 Which city from the list below is closest to the equator?

A New York

B Madrid

C Chicago

D Rome

589 If Mandarin Chinese is the world's most spoken language, where does Spanish rank?

A 2nd

B 3rd

C 4th

D 5th

590 What river flows through Warsaw in Poland?

A Dnieper

B Oder

C Danube

D Vistula

591 Which African desert is home to Dallol, the officially hottest average place on earth?

A Kalahari Desert   C Sahara Desert
B Danakil Desert   D Guban Desert

592 To the nearest 1000 miles, what is the distance between New York and Rio De Janeiro?

A 3000 miles   C 5000 miles
B 4000 miles   D 6000 miles

593 What is the name of a point where two rivers flow to create a larger river?

A Junction   C Merger
B Confluence   D Tributary

594 In which U.S. state is the Death Valley located?

A California   C Arizona
B Nevada   D New Mexico

595 In which European country can I find the city of Kosice?

A Czech Republic   C Slovenia
B Poland   D Slovakia

596 With an area of just 0.81 square miles (2.2km^2), what is the second smallest country in the world?

A Vatican City   C San Marino
B Liechtenstein   D Monaco

597 What is the capital of the French region of Occitanie?

A Perpignan   C Toulouse
B Montpellier   D Avignon

598 How many stars appear on the Brazilian flag?

A 8   C 26
B 18   D 42

599 In which African country can you find the cities of Kano and Ibadan?

A Nigeria   C Ghana
B Kenya   D Tanzania

600 The Ellora Caves, a UNESCO listed religious site, is located in which Asian country?

A Thailand   C Vietnam
B India   D Malaysia

/20

601 Hamad International Airport is the only airport of which Asian country?

A Kuwait
B Brunei

C Azerbaijan
D Qatar

602 What is the capital of Belize?

A Belmopan
B San Salvador

C Merida
D Tegucigalpa

603 What is the largest island belonging to the USA?

A Puerto Rico
B Hawaii

C Long Island
D Kodiak Island

604 To the nearest 1000 miles, what is the distance between Cape Town and London?

A 4000 miles
B 6000 miles

C 8000 miles
D 10,000 miles

605 True or False, the landlocked country of Lesotho, entirely bordered by South Africa, is the smallest in Africa?

606 In which U.S. state are the towns of Boise and Twin Falls located?

A Wyoming
B Idaho

C Montana
D Utah

607 Which U.S. state flag features the French tricolor as part of it's design?

A Illinois
B Louisiana

C Iowa
D Missouri

608 Which city could one find the San Siro stadium?

A Rome
B Milan

C Madrid
D Malaga

609 What is the capital of the Spanish community of Andalusia?

A Cordoba
B Seville

C Malaga
D Valencia

610 Eivissa is the local name for which popular tourist island?

A Tenerife
B Mallorca

C Ibiza
D Rhodes

611 Which country may access Lake Victoria, Lake
Tanganyika and Lake Malawi within it's borders?

A Tanzania   **C** Kenya
B Malawi   **D** Democratic Republic Of Congo

612 What is the largest settlement in the Greek region of
Macedonia?

A Larissa   **C** Ptolemaida
B Kavala   **D** Thessaloniki

613 The towns of Namibe and Lobito may be found in
which African country?

A South Africa   **C** Angola
B Namibia   **D** Botswana

614 What is the largest island of the country of Wales?

A Isle of Man   **C** Anglesey
B Arran   **D** Holyhead

615 The Lake District national park and England's highest
mountain is located in which county?

A Northumberland   **C** Lancashire
B Yorkshire   **D** Cumbria

616 What is the only South American country to have
Dutch as an official language?

A Guyana   **C** Suriname
B Brazil   **D** Venezuela

617 What is the longest river located in Spain?

A Po   **C** Ebro
B Tagus   **D** Douro

618 Xidan and Dongcheng are districts of which city?

A Shanghai   **C** Hong Kong
B Beijing   **D** Guangzhou

619 What country from the Australia & Oceania continent is
closest to the Philippines?

A Micronesia   **C** Palau
B Papua New Guinea   **D** Tonga

620 McCarran International Airport serves which U.S. city?

A Los Angeles   **C** Sacramento
B Reno   **D** Las Vegas

621 The Taureg people inhabit large areas of which desert?

A Gobi Desert   C Sahara Desert
B Arabian Desert   D Patagonian Desert

622 Cork in Ireland is the largest city of which Irish province?

A Munster   C Connacht
B Leinster   D Ulster

623 The Iguazu falls is a waterfall lying between which two South American countries?

A Argentina & Brazil   C Peru & Brazil
B Venezuela & Brazil   D Bolivia & Brazil

624 How many sovereign country's flag are only blue and yellow?

A 2   C 5
B 3   D 7

625 To the nearest 1000 miles, what is the distance between the Russian cities of St. Petersburg and Vladivostok?

A 2000 miles   C 6000 miles
B 4000 miles   D 8000 miles

626 What is the capital of Eritrea?

A Afar   C Addis Ababa
B Mitsiwa   D Asmara

627 The River Niger in Africa crosses through the capital cities of Niger and which other African country?

A Burkina Faso   C Mali
B Nigeria   D Benin

628 Mahajanga and Antisiranana are towns located in which African country?

A Seychelles   C Mozambique
B Comoros   D Madagascar

629 Excluding Jerusalem, what is Israel's largest city by population?

A Bethlehem   C Nazareth
B Tel Aviv   D Haifa

630 How many Greek islands are inhabited, to the nearest 100?

A 100   C 400
B 200   D 800

631 Yaba and Igbobi are districts of which African city?
A Kinshasa
B Nairobi
C Johannesburg
D Lagos

632 Bishkek is the capital of which Central Asian country?
A Tajikistan
B Uzbekistan
C Kyrgyzstan
D Turkmenistan

633 What is the Maori (native) name for New Zealand's highest peak, Mt. Cook?
A Tititea
B Aoraki
C Te Anau
D Wanaka

634 Mt. Fitz Roy is a spectacular mountain found on the border of which two countries?
A USA & Canada
B Argentina & Chile
C Papua New Guinea & Indonesia
D South Africa & Botswana

635 Which U.S. state has the most populous capital?
A Massachusetts
B Arizona
C Colorado
D Texas

636 The British seaside town of Bournemouth is found in which county?
A Hampshire
B Jersey
C Dorset
D Sussex

637 The towns of Cabo San Lucas and La Paz may be found in which Mexican state?
A Baja California Sur
B Jalisco
C Sinaloa
D Baja California

638 The coldest ever temperature recorded on the Earth's surface was measured at which Antarctic research station?
A Scott-Amundsen Station
B Vostok Station
C Queen Elizabeth Station
D Troll Station

639 Liechtenstein is a country sandwiched between Switzerland and which other country?
A Austria
B Italy
C France
D Germany

640 Spain's highest mountain, Teide, is located on which island?
A Menorca
B Fuerteventura
C Lanzarote
D Tenerife

641 Bloemfontein and Durban are cities located in which country?
A Namibia
B Suriname
C Netherlands
D South Africa

642 Amboseli National Park may be found in which African country?
A Tanzania
B Kenya
C South Africa
D Botswana

643 Bari, facing the Adriatic Sea, is the capital of which region of Italy?
A Lombardy
B Apulia
C Tuscany
D Abruzzo

644 After Stockholm, what is Sweden's next largest city by population?
A Helsingborg
B Gothenburg
C Kalmar
D Malmo

645 Finland gained independence from which country in 1917?
A Sweden
B Denmark
C Kalmar Union
D Russian Empire

646 To the nearest 1000 miles, what is the length of the Andes mountain range?
A 1000 miles
B 2000 miles
C 3000 miles
D 4000 miles

647 Mumbai is the largest city of which Indian state?
A Gujarat
B Goa
C Karnataka
D Maharashtra

648 What is Germany's busiest airport?
A Munich Airport
B Frankfurt Airport
C Berlin Airport
D Hamburg Airport

649 What is the capital of Tuscany in Italy?
A Rome
B Turin
C Genova
D Florence

650 What is the highest mountain in Bhutan?
A Kula Kangri
B Kangchenjunga
C Gangkhar Puensum
D Khan Tengri

651 How high is the world's tallest waterfall, Angel Falls?
A 379 metres (1243 feet)　　　C 779 metres (2556 feet)
B 579 metres (1900 feet)　　　D 979 metres (3212 feet)

652 What is the demonym of the native residents of the Cuban capital, Havana?
A Habano　　　C Habanero
B Cubana　　　D Havanero

653 What is the name of Jamaica's highest peak?
A Blue Mountain Peak　　　C Garvey Peak
B Bustamante Peak　　　D Mt. Montego

654 What is the name of the largest island belonging to The Bahamas?
A Abaco　　　C Andros Island
B Grand Bahama　　　D Great Inagua

655 The Andaman and Nicobar Islands belong to which country?
A India　　　C United Kingdom
B Indonesia　　　D Myanmar

656 What city hosted the 2000 Olympic Games?
A Athens　　　C Sydney
B Moscow　　　D Paris

657 Tripoli, the capital of Libya, derives from the Greek meaning of what?
A Three Lands　　　C Three Residences
B Three Cities　　　D Three People

658 What is the highest mountain of Iceland?
A Snæfell　　　C Herðubreið
B Hvannadalshnúkur　　　D Hofsjökull

659 In which country would you find the zen temple of Ginkaku-Ji?
A Thailand　　　C Japan
B South Korea　　　D China

660 Bodga Peak, the highest mountain in the Bodga Shan Mountain range, is found in which country?
A China　　　C India
B Russia　　　D Pakistan

661 Which country has the most natural lakes in the world?

A Russia

B Sweden

C Canada

D China

662 What is China's largest export product?

A Refined Metals

B Petroleum Oil

C Electrical Equipment

D Pharmaceuticals

663 What is the official currency used in Botswana?

A Dollar

B Rand

C Pula

D Pound

664 What country has the highest average altitude in the world?

A Bolivia

B Andorra

C Bhutan

D Rwanda

665 What is the highest mountain of the Caribbean islands?

A Pico Neblina

B Pico Duarte

C Bustamante Peak

D Pico Turquino

666 What is the capital of the U.S. state of West Virginia?

A Annapolis

B Richmond

C Morgantown

D Charleston

667 What is the UK's most southerly National Park?

A Exmoor

B Dartmoor

C Peak District

D New Forest

668 The Belgian city of Antwerp lies of which river?

A Rhine

B Scheldt

C Seine

D Meuse

669 The cities of Chongjin and Hamhung are located in which country?

A China

B South Korea

C North Korea (DPRK)

D Japan

670 Which country has the oldest continually used flag in the world?

A United Kingdom

B Denmark

C Portugal

D Spain

671 Which country listed below is largest in land area?

A Egypt
B France
C Turkey
D Chile

672 Incheon International Airport is the largest airport of what country?

A Taiwan
B Brunei
C South Korea
D North Korea

673 What is the capital of Laos?

A Phnom Penh
B Savannakhet
C Vientiane
D Pakse

674 What is the highest mountain of the Ural mountain range?

A Mt. Narodnaya
B Manaraga
C Belukha Mountain
D Koryaksky

675 Which U.S. state is immediately north of Arkansas?

A Oklahoma
B Nebraska
C Kansas
D Missouri

676 What country from the list below is largest?

A Spain
B Kenya
C Madagascar
D Iraq

677 What country is home to the largest deposits of diamonds in the world?

A South Africa
B Russia
C Sierra Leone
D Tanzania

678 What country is the largest producer of Aluminum in the world?

A China
B Chile
C United States
D Australia

679 What German state completely surrounds the city state of Berlin?

A Mecklenburg-Vorpommern
B Potsdam
C Saxony-Anhalt
D Brandenburg

680 What country from the list below is largest?

A Germany
B Japan
C Norway
D Poland

681 The Great Dividing Range is a mountain range found in which country?
A Australia
B Canada
C United Kingdom
D New Zealand

682 The Valdivian Forest is a large temperate rainforest found in which country?
A Armenia
B Italy
C Chile
D Russia

683 What is the capital of the U.S. state of Oregon?
A Eugene
B Tacoma
C Salem
D Portland

684 Westfalenstadion is a football stadium loacted in which German city?
A Munich
B Westfalen
C Dortmund
D Hamburg

685 What river flows through the Chinese city of Chengdu?
A Yellow River
B Fuhe River
C Huai River
D Xiangjiang River

686 Edinburgh of the Seven Seas is the largest settlement of which island?
A Saint Helena
B Sandwich Islands
C Tristan De Cunha
D South Georgia

687 What is the name of the highest active volcano on Earth?
A Ojos Del Salado
B Mt. Elbrus
C Aconcagua
D Pico De Orizaba

688 What is the name of Estonia, in Estonian?
A Esktva
B Esstoniya
C Eesti
D Estonia

689 What is the romanized name of Montenegro, in Montenegrin?
A Montnigra
B Crna Gora
C Montnigroiya
D Crnaiya

690 What is the capital of the Australian state of Tasmania?
A Tasman Town
B Launceston
C Hobart
D Oban

691 What is the largest city by population of Morocco?
A Tangier   C Casablanca
B Marrakech   D Fez

692 According the Koppen classification, an Oceanic climate, such as the climate of the UK, is defined by no month averaging a temperature below freezing or above what temperature?
A 15°C (50°F)   C 20°C (68°F)
B 18°C (64.4°F)   D 22°C (71.6°F)

693 After Istanbul and Ankara, what is the next largest city of Turkey?
A Izmir   C Samsun
B Antalya   D Adana

694 What country from the list below is largest?
A Colombia   C Bolivia
B Peru   D Venezuela

695 What is the capital of the French region of Normandy?
A Le Havre   C Caen
B Cherbourg   D Rouen

696 What is the official currency used in Peru?
A Bolivar   C Peso
B Sol   D Real

697 What animal is depicted on the Mexican coat of arms?
A Wolf   C Eagle
B Lion   D Hawk

698 What territory below is the smallest in size?
A Greenland   C Argentina
B India   D Algeria

699 The UNESCO world heritage site of Ha Long Bay is located in which country?
A Thailand   C Vietnam
B Philippines   D China

700 Machu Picchu was a citadel built by which civilisation?
A Aztec   C Inca
B Cambeba   D Maya

/20

701 The Serengeti National Park is a well known national park found in which country?

A Kenya   C Central African Republic
B Nigeria   D Tanzania

702 What country from the list below is largest?

A Sri Lanka   C Netherlands
B Belgium   D Ireland

703 What is the shortest distance between mainland Russia and mainland Alaska?

A 3 miles   C 51 miles
B 22 miles   D 85 miles

704 After megacities of Sao Paulo and Rio De Janeiro, whats the next largest city by population in Brazil?

A Porto Alegre   C Brasilia
B Belo Horizonte   D Recife

705 The towns of Bitola and Prilep are located in which country?

A Kosovo   C Montenegro
B North Macedonia   D Serbia

706 Which is the longest bi-national border from those listed below?

A India - China   C Russia - China
B India - Bangladesh   D Russia - Mongolia

707 Which country would one visit to view the impact crater that caused the extinction of dinosaurs?

A Guatemala   C United States
B Mexico   D Honduras

708 What is the world's oldest active volcano?

A Mauna Kea   C Mt. Etna
B Mt. Fuji   D Mt. Olympus

709 What sea, bordering the Atlantic Ocean, is the westernmost within the Mediterranean Sea?

A Balearic Sea   C Ionian Sea
B Tyrrhenian Sea   D Alboran Sea

710 Which U.S. state has the most miles of river flowing through?

A Nebraska   C Florida
B Alaska   D Mississippi

711 Sitting on the River Ganges, what is regarded as India's oldest city?
A Calcutta   C Varanasi
B New Delhi   D Patna

712 The Zagros Mountains may be found in which country?
A Greece   C Kazakhstan
B Iran   D Saudi Arabia

713 The majority of the Sierra Nevada mountain range is found in which U.S. state?
A Arizona   C Utah
B Nevada   D California

714 What is the capital of the Canadian province of British Columbia?
A Vancouver   C Victoria
B Abbotsford   D Calgary

715 After Sydney Harbor, what is the world's second largest natural harbor?
A San Francisco Harbor   C Kotor Harbor
B Rio De Janeiro Harbor   D Poole Harbor

716 What African nation has the largest amount of pyramids?
A Sudan   C Libya
B Egypt   D Tunisia

717 Which country was scenes from Star War's Tatooine filmed at?
A Mexico   C Saudi Arabia
B Tunisia   D Algeria

718 What is France's largest national park?
A Ecrins national park   C Vanoise national park
B Pyrenees national park   D Alpine national park

719 What is the oldest city in the world?
A Jerusalem   C Damascus
B Bethlehem   D Jericho

720 What is the capital of the Canadian province of Quebec?
A Sherbrooke   C Ottawa-Gatineau
B Quebec City   D Montreal

THE ULTIMATE GEOGRAPHY
QUIZ BOOK

THE
ANSWERS

STILL HAVE SOME QUIZZING LEFT INSIDE YOU?

FOR A FEW EXTRA BONUS QUESTIONS, HEAD TO
PAGE 96!

1 B - Egypt
2 C - Australia & Oceania (Oceania)
3 D - Sea Of Japan
4 A - 3000 miles
5 C - Calypso Deep
6 B - Greece
7 D - Pennsylvania
8 A - Pacific Ocean
9 A - The British Empire
10 A - The Netherlands
11 C - Denmark
12 D - 10
13 B - New Guinea
14 C - Moskva River
15 D - Brazil (via French Guiana)
16 A - Riyal
17 A - India, Nepal, Mauritius
18 C - 3 (Malaysia, Papua New Guinea, Timor-Leste)
19 B - Argentina
20 A - Birmingham
21 D - Naples
22 B - Indian Ocean
23 C - M
24 A - Drachma
25 B - Bullet Train
26 C - Montevideo of Uruguay
27 A - Canada
28 D - Seine River
29 B - Harry Potter
30 D - Bulgaria
31 B - Stockholm
32 B - District of Columbia
33 C - Jordan
34 A - Tropic Of Cancer
35 C - Vietnam
36 D - Louisiana
37 B - Queensland
38 C - Zimbabwe
39 A - Greenland
40 D - United Kingdom

41 C - 5000 miles
42 C - Yangtze
43 A - South Dakota
44 B - Dallas
45 C - Steppe
46 A - Mauritius
47 B - 3rd
48 C - 1880s
49 C - 26 countries
50 D - Antarctica
51 C - 3
52 A - Loch Ness
53 D - London St. Pancras
54 B - 10 (10 provinces and 3 territories)
55 D - 4 (Guinea, Guinea-Bissau, Equatorial Guinea, Papua New Guinea)
56 C - 11
57 A - Cantonese
58 B - Cyrillic
59 D - Cypriot
60 C - Catalan
61 B - Persian Gulf / Arabian Gulf
62 C - Burkina Faso
63 A - Tanzania, Uganda, Kenya
64 A - 1
65 C - Venezuela
66 D - Lake Huron
67 B - Frankfort
68 C - New York State
69 C - Iqaluit
70 A - Giza
71 B - Spain
72 A - Honshu
73 C - 18,000
74 D - Hindi
75 B - Bangladesh
76 B - 1917
77 A - Bay Stater
78 D - Romania
79 C - Wyoming
80 B - 5m (16ft)

81 C - Transform Plate Boundary
82 A - North Carolina
83 B - La Rinconada
84 D - Colombia (Christopher Columbus)
85 B - Turin
86 A - South America
87 C - Brooklyn & Queens
88 C - 9
89 A - Democratic Republic Of Congo
90 D - La Paz, Bolivia
91 B - France & Spain
92 D - Saudi Arabia
93 C - 15
94 B - Dili
95 B - Western Australia
96 A - Norway
97 C - Ecuador
98 A - River Severn
99 D - Lake Baikal
100 A - Missouri River
101 C - China & Mongolia
102 D - Pakistan
103 B - 5
104 D - Brazil
105 C - Chile
106 B - 3 (excluding Malaysia and Russia - these countries aren't 'passed')
107 C - Russia
108 D - New Caledonia
109 A - South Africa
110 B - Indonesia
111 B - 1901
112 D - 50 times
113 B - Bali
114 C - Ulaanbaatar
115 D - Uttar Pradesh
116 B - 5
117 A - Lithuania & Poland
118 A - Caribbean
119 C - West Indies (Antilles excludes islands associated with the Caribbean)
120 B - Haiti

121 A - Ile De France
122 C - Geneva
123 D - Dufourspitze
124 B - Po Valley
125 A - Porto-Novo
126 C - 54
127 B - Africa, Asia, Europe
128 D - The Bosphorus
129 C - Republic of China
130 C - Turkey
131 B - 1870s
132 B - Dubai
133 D - Iraq
134 B - Great Pyramids of Giza (the rest also exist but are not regarded as ancient)
135 A - Poland
136 C - Chad
137 A - Cote D'Ivoire
138 D - Red
139 D - Nepal
140 B - Rhode Island
141 B - Green
142 C - Green, Yellow, Red
143 B - Poland
144 A - Isle of Lewis
145 D - Torshavn
146 A - Isle of Wight
147 B - 26 miles
148 C - Germany, Switzerland, Austria
149 B - 6 (Germany, Switzerland, Austria, Liechtenstein, Belgium, Luxembourg)
150 B - China (legitimacy disputed by Taiwan)
151 A - Portugal
152 B - Oil
153 C - Shanghai
154 B - 10200m
155 A - Musala
156 C - Singapore
157 D - Monaco
158 A - Bosnia & Herzegovina
159 C - Mulhacen
160 D - Peseta

161 A - Senegal
162 C - Ethiopia
163 B - Turkey
164 D - Tunisia
165 C - Russia
166 D - French Polynesia
167 C - Papua New Guinea
168 B - Middle East
169 A - Mohe City
170 C - North Korea
171 B - 14
172 D - Mt. Etna
173 A - Utqiagvik (formerly named Barrows)
174 B - Himalayas
175 C - India
176 B - 1 (Israel)
177 C - Rufiyaa
178 A - Maltese
179 B - 10
180 C - Muscat
181 B - Cape Town
182 C - Chennai
183 D - Southampton
184 C - Oahu
185 A - Serbia
186 B - 1992
187 D - 2011
188 C - Australia & Oceania
189 B - Africa
190 D - North America
191 D - St. Petersburg
192 C - Volgograd
193 B - Mikhael Gorbachev
194 A - Franc
195 C - Montgomery
196 D - Svizzera
197 C - Frankreich
198 B - Etats-Unis
199 D - Germany
200 C - Hargeisa

201 B - Yemen
202 A - Africa
203 A - Saudi Arabia
204 C - Lesotho
205 D - South Africa
206 C - Ethiopia
207 B - Ukraine
208 A - Maputo
209 C - Arizona
210 C - 2
211 D - Quintana Roo
212 D - 1800 feet, 600 metres
213 A - Australia & Oceania
214 C - Windsor
215 B - Chihuahua
216 D - 13
217 C - Fernsehrturm
218 B - Sevastopol
219 B - Haiti & Dominican Republic
220 A - Sargasso Sea
221 C - South China Sea
222 B - Indian Ocean
223 D - Attu Island
224 B - 90 miles
225 A - Arctic and Pacific Ocean
226 C - 12,430 miles
227 A - Asuncion
228 D - Afghanistan
229 D - Tajikistan
230 C - Mecca
231 C - Laurasia & Gondwanaland
232 C - 60th parallel south
233 A - Edirne
234 D - Borneo
235 B - Hungary
236 C - Gokkceada
237 A - Palestine
238 C - Gulf Of Aqaba/Eilat
239 B - Congo River
240 B - Lithuania

241 A - U-Bahn
242 D - Algarve
243 B - Czech Republic
244 B - Monte Pico
245 C - Portuguese
246 D - East Germany (German Democratic Republic)
247 A - Hainan
248 C - Dagestan
249 C - 2
250 C - Tigris
251 B - 22%
252 D - Darwin, Australia
253 A - Alaska
254 A - France
255 D - China
256 B - Tainos
257 C - Helsinki
258 D - 8
259 A - Honshu
260 C - Moscow
261 B - 8
262 C - 12%
263 C - 12%
264 A - 1
265 C - Sicily
266 B - IKA
267 B - Papeete
268 D - Hawai'i
269 C - 9
270 B - 100 miles
271 A - Zealand
272 C - Finland
273 A & C - Caucasus and Urals
274 B - 7 (Except Alberta, Saskatchewan and Manitoba)!
275 A - South and North Korea
276 C - Baffin Island
277 D - Sakhalin
278 B - Lambert-Fisher glacier
279 C - Port-Aux-Francais
280 C - 60th parallel south

281 C - Amundsen-Scott Station
282 B - Norway
283 D - Denmark
284 D - 1958
285 C - 6
286 A - Somalia
287 D - Jewish Autonomous Oblast (created in the aftermath of WW2)
288 D - 10
289 A - Siberia
290 B - Mojave Desert
291 C - Yukon & Northwest
292 B - Northern Territories
293 D - Java
294 D - Andorra
295 B - Austria
296 C - Norway
297 A - New Orleans
298 C - Slovenia
299 B - Outer Hebrides
300 A - Lhasa
301 D - Neva River
302 C - Australia & Oceania (Oceania)
303 D - Venice
304 D - 1860s
305 B - Algeria
306 D - Gavdos
307 C - China
308 C - Iran
309 A - Nakhchivan
310 B - Hrvatska
311 D - Shqiperia
312 C - Magyarország
313 A - Ruwenzori
314 Northern
315 C - 5
316 B - Helsinki & Tallinn
317 C - Poland & Slovakia
318 B - Greece
319 D - Caprivi Strip
320 C - Punjab

321 Fiji
322 C - Ultra Prominent Mountains
323 D - The native people of Easter Island
324 A - Melanesia
325 B - Polynesia
326 D - Lake Erie & Ontario
327 B - Minnesota
328 C - Kiribati
329 B - Australia
330 B - New Mexico
331 B - 2
332 C - Taipei-101
333 A - Lake Lugano
334 D - Italy
335 A - 1790s
336 B - 9 miles
337 C - Galicia
338 B - Algeria
339 D - Vancouver Island
340 B - 45th parallel
341 A - 6 (Tunisia and South Africa excluded as they are not 'passed').
342 B & D - Ecuador & Chile
343 D - Turkey
344 C - Angkor Wat
345 B - Singapore
346 C - Brussels
347 B - Jutland
348 B - Transnistria
349 A - Siswati
350 C - St. Lucia
351 C - Trinidad and Tobago
352 B - Latin Alphabet
353 A - Equatorial Guinea
354 C - United Mexican States
355 C - 4 (China, Cuba, Laos, Vietnam)
356 A - Emirate of Grenada
357 C - 1997
358 C - 4 (Nunavut, Manitoba, Ontario, Quebec)
359 B - Missouri
360 D - 8

361 C - 10°C (50°F)
362 C - 3
363 D - Kazakhstan-Russia
364 False
365 B - Quintana Roo
366 A - USA
367 A - Netherlands (province of Zeeland)
368 D - 11
369 B - 18°C (64.4°F)
370 D - Hinduism
371 D - Switzerland
372 B - North Carolina
373 D - 4 (all but Lake Ontario)
374 A - Urumqi
375 C - Lampedusa
376 C - Senegal
377 B - Benguela Current
378 D - Copenhagen
379 B - 12
380 B - Indonesia
381 A - Nicaragua
382 C - Detroit
383 C - Colorado & Wyoming
384 A - Dublin
385 C - Banking
386 B - Japanese
387 D - Sea Of Japan
388 B - Luzon
389 C - Monrovia
390 D - Red Sea
391 C - 12
392 C - Bantustan
393 A - Myanmar
394 C - Riau Islands
395 A - Alert
396 B - 14
397 D - Germany
398 B - Munchen
399 D - Ragusa
400 B - Zante

401 A - Peloponnesse
402 C - Mt. Elbrus (5642m)
403 D - Iceland
404 A - Tongass
405 B - Beb-El-Mandeb
406 D - Flanders
407 A - Othonoi
408 D - Atlantic Ocean (Sea of Azov is a marginal sea of the Black Sea)
409 B - Kazakhstan & Uzbekistan
410 C - SADR (Sahrawi Arab Democratic Republic)
411 D - Arkansas
412 B - Minnesota & South Dakota
413 D - 3 (France, Spain, Algeria)
414 C - 6 (UTC-1 Cape Verde to UTC+4 Seychelles)
415 B - Seychelles
416 A - Tanzania
417 C - Tamil Nadu
418 B - Iraq
419 C - Switzerland
420 A - Mashhad
421 C - Nauru
422 C - 16 (up to 18 if you count maroon)
423 B - Canada
424 B - Lithuania
425 C - Ubangi
426 D - Norway
427 B - Patagonian Desert
428 C - USA - from Polar to Tropical
429 A - Kathmandu
430 B - 5 (Switzerland, Austria, France, Spain, Italy)
431 A - Arctic Ocean (north of Russia)
432 C - Belgium
433 C - Ethiopia
434 D - Cook Strait
435 B - Cote D'Ivoire & Guinea
436 A - Russia
437 D - 2 and a half hours.
438 B - Poland
439 D - 50%
440 B & C - Argentina & Uruguay

441 C - New Guinea
442 D - Peking
443 A - Lithuania, Latvia and Estonia
444 C - Sorbonne
445 B - Egypt
446 C - Oxford
447 D - Florida
448 C - Jordan
449 C - M25
450 D - Interstate 95
451 B - Lake Como
452 B - California
453 D - Santa Monica & Chicago
454 A - Paris
455 C - FC Barcelona
456 C - 4 (Germany, Austria, Switzerland and the USA)
457 D - Quebec City
458 C - Battle of Waterloo
459 B - El Salvador
460 C - Lincoln Cathedral
461 A - Nuuk
462 D - Russia
463 C - Arizona
464 B - Winnipeg
465 D - River Cam
466 D - West
467 B - Kyoto
468 C - Virginia
469 D - Lebanon
470 A - Texas
471 C - Indonesia
472 B - Liberia
473 C - Uluru
474 A - Kalahari
475 C - Egypt
476 A - Toubkal
477 B - Italy
478 D - Brazil with Pico De Neblina (2995m)
479 D - Japan
480 B - Rio Grande

481 C - 7000
482 D - South Korea
483 C - Halla-San (1947m)
484 B - 5959m (19,551 feet)
485 B - Dead Sea
486 B - Pacific Ocean
487 D - Malta
488 C - France
489 A - Kazakhstan
490 C - Switzerland
491 B - Pittsburgh
492 C - Miami
493 D - Japan
494 C - Canada
495 A - Belgium
496 B - Belarus
497 B - Blue and Yellow
498 D - Oxbow Lake
499 C - Vaduz
500 B - Baltimore
501 D - Tokyo
502 C - Petroleum oil
503 B - Massachusetts
504 A - Wyomingite
505 A - Hokkaido
506 D - Shanghai
507 C - Hong Kong
508 D - Tajikistan
509 B - Lima
510 B - The Humboldt current
511 C - The Semien Mountains
512 A - Madagascar
513 D - Islamabad
514 C - Halifax
515 C - Croatia
516 B - Romance Language
517 D - Uralic Language
518 A - Cameroon
519 C - Renminbi
520 B - Reykjavik

521 D - Brooklyn Bridge
522 B - Austin
523 C - 4th
524 B - 3 (New Guinea, Hawaii, Borneo)
525 D - Maldives
526 C - Invercargill
527 C - 10 times (604mm London vs. 6400mm Milford Sound)
528 B - Washington
529 A - Pest
530 C - Eiffel Tower
531 B - Frédéric Auguste Bartholdi
532 C - By Camel
533 A - Texas
534 D - Tobacco & Sugar
535 C - El Paso
536 A - Italy
537 D - Napoleon Bonaparte
538 B - Bhutan
539 B - Saffron
540 C - Nordic Cross
541 B - Japan
542 D - Bavaria
543 A - Motor Vehicles
544 C - Sami
545 A - Milan
546 B - Naples
547 C - Bonn
548 D - Indonesia
549 C - Vancouver
550 D - Azerbaijan
551 A - Mt. Elbrus (5642m)
552 B - Kazakhstan
553 C - 10,000 miles
554 C - 3000 miles
555 A - IST
556 D - Montana
557 C - Florence
558 A - Italy
559 C - Lake Titicaca
560 D - New Zealand

561 B - Tijuana
562 A - Phou Bia (2818m)
563 C - Noumea
564 B - Australia
565 D - Italy
566 D - 11,000 miles
567 C - Lestho
568 B - 2 (California and Tennessee)
569 True
570 D - Brazzaville
571 B - Kazakhstan
572 B - Constantinople
573 D - Mali
574 D - Shanghai
575 A - River Delta
576 B - River Elbe
577 A - 300 miles
578 C - 11
579 B - Nigeria
580 B - Dubai
581 A - Norway
582 C - Monaco
583 D - China
584 B - Netherlands
585 C - Central Line
586 A - Funafuti
587 B - Lebanon
588 B - Madrid
589 C - 4th
590 D - Vistula
591 B - Danakil Desert
592 C - 5000 miles
593 B - Confluence
594 B - California
595 D - Slovakia
596 D - Monaco
597 C - Toulouse
598 C - 26
599 A - Nigeria
600 B - India

601 D - Qatar
602 A - Belmopan
603 B - Hawaii
604 C - 8000 miles
605 False - Seychelles is the smallest.
606 B - Idaho
607 C - Iowa
608 B - Milan
609 B - Seville
610 C - Ibiza
611 A - Tanzania
612 D - Thessaloniki
613 C - Angola
614 C - Anglesey
615 D - Cumbria
616 C - Suriname
617 B - Tagus
618 B - Beijing
619 C - Palau
620 D - Las Vegas
621 C - Sahara Desert
622 A - Munster
623 A - Argentina & Brazil
624 C - 5 (Sweden, Ukraine, Kazakhstan, Bosnia & Herzegovina, Palau)
625 C - 6000 miles
626 D - Asmara
627 C - Mali
628 D - Madagascar
629 B - Tel Aviv
630 B - 200
631 D - Lagos
632 C - Kyrgyzstan
633 B - Aoraki
634 B - Argentina & Chile
635 B - Arizona
636 C - Dorset
637 A - Baja California Sur
638 B - Vostok Station
639 A - Austria
640 D - Tenerife

641 D - South Africa
642 B - Kenya
643 B - Apulia
644 A - Pacific Ocean
645 D - The Russian Empire
646 D - 4000 miles
647 D - Maharashtra
648 B - Frankfurt Airport
649 D - Tuscany
650 C - Gangkhar Puensum (7570m)
651 D - 979 metres (3212 feet)
652 C - Habanero
653 A - Blue Mountain Peak (2256m)
654 C - Andros Island
655 A - India
656 C - Sydney
657 B - Three Cities
658 B - Hvannadalshnúkur (2110m)
659 C - Japan
660 A - China
661 C - Canada
662 C - Electrical Equipment
663 C - Pula
664 C - Bhutan
665 B - Pico Duarte (Dominican Republic)
666 D - Charleston
667 B - Dartmoor
668 B - Scheldt
669 C - North Korea (DPRK)
670 B - Denmark
671 A - Egypt
672 C - South Korea
673 C - Vientiane
674 A - Mt. Narodnaya (1895m)
675 D - Missouri
676 C - Madagascar
677 B - Russia
678 A - China
679 D - Brandenburg
680 B - Japan

681 A - Australia
682 C - Chile
683 C - Denmark
684 C - Dortmund
685 B - Egypt
686 C - Tristan De Cunha
687 A - Ojos Del Salado (6893m)
688 C - Eesti
689 B - Crna Gora
690 C - Hobart
691 C - Casablanca
692 D - 22°C (71.6°F)
693 A - Izmir
694 B - Peru
695 C - Denmark
696 B - Sol
697 C - Eagle
698 A - Greenland
699 C - Vietnam
700 C - Inca
701 D - Tanzania
702 D - Ireland
703 C - 51 miles
704 A - Belo Horizonte
705 B - North Macedonia
706 B - India - Bangladesh
707 C - Mexico
708 C - Mt. Etna (first eruption was 1500BC)
709 D - Alboran Sea
710 A - Nebraska
711 C - Varanasi
712 B - Iran
713 D - California
714 C - Victoria
715 D - Poole Harbor
716 A - Sudan
717 B - Tunisia
718 C - Vanoise national park
719 C - Damascus
720 B - Quebec City

B1 **The basalt columns of the Giant's Causeway in Northern Ireland are mostly what shape?**
A Pentagonal
B Hexagonal
C Octagonal
D Decagonal

B2 **What river forms the state border of 5 U.S. states, including Indiana, Ohio and Kentucky?**
A Tennessee
B Ohio
C Wabash
D Kentucky

B3 **What is Papua New Guinea's largest export by earnings?**
A Oil
B Minerals
C Timber
D Food

B4 **How many countries does Iran border?**
A 5
B 7
C 9
D 11

B5 **After Toronto and Montreal, what is the third most populous city in Canada?**
A Calgary
B Mississauga
C Winnipeg
D Vancouver

B6 **After the U.S. Dollar and Euro, what is the next largest traded currency by volume?**
A Chinese Renminbi
B Pound Sterling
C Japanese Yen
D Australian Dollar

B7 **The Nile Delta extends how long down the Mediterranean coastline?**
A 50 miles (80km)
B 150 miles (240km)
C 250 miles (400km)
D 400 miles (640km)

B8 **How many U.S. states are named after native American tribes?**
A 6
B 16
C 26
D 36

B9 **What flower is Japan's coat of arms?**
A Chrysanthemum
B Mugunghwa (Rose Of Sharon)
C Cherry Blossom
D Plum Blossom

B10 **Roughly what percentage of The Netherland's land falls below sea level?**
A 2%
B 7%
C 17%
D 27%

B11 **The Dead Sea is Earth's lowest elevation on land. How much below sea level is it's lowest point to the nearest metre?**

A 145m (476ft)   C 357m (1171ft)
B 223m (732ft)   D 431m (1412ft)

B12 **What is the largest lake in Europe?**

A Lake Ladoga   C Lake Baikal
B Lake Balaton   D Lake Onega

B13 **If one were to sail from Varna to Odessa, which sea would they cross?**

A Caspian Sea   C Baltic Sea
B Black Sea   D Mediterranean Sea

B14 **The Abominable Snowman is a folklore creature of which world region?**

A Siberia   C Himalayas
B Andes   D Japan

B15 **Which of the below is not a Celtic Nation?**

A Wales   C Cornwall
B Brittany   D Cumbria

B16 **How many South American country high points exceed 6000m?**

A 3   C 5
B 4   D 6

B17 **What is the national flower of India?**

A Lily   C Jasmine
B Lotus Flower   D Saffron

B18 **Which of these Canary Islands is closest to the African mainland?**

A Fuerteventura   C Gran Canaria
B Tenerife   D Lanzarote

B19 **Kiev lies on which river?**

A Danube   C Don
B Dnieper   D Pripyat

B20 **Which of these country high points is closest to to equator?**

A Mount Chimborazo   C Puncak Jaya
B Mount Kilimanjaro   D Mount Stanley

B1 B - Hexagonal
B2 B - Ohio
B3 A - Minerals
B4 B - 7
B5 D - Vancouver
B6 C - Japanese Yen
B7 B - 150 miles (240km)
B8 C - 26
B9 A - Chrysanthemum
B10 C - 17%
B11 D - 431m (1412ft)
B12 A - Lake Ladoga
B13 B - Black Sea
B14 C - Himalayas
B15 D - Cumbria
B16 C - 5 (Argentina, Chile, Ecuador, Peru, Bolivia)
B17 B - Lotus Flower
B18 A - Fuerteventura
B19 B - Dnieper
B20 D - Mount Stanley!

Made in the USA
Middletown, DE
17 December 2020

28932745R00059